Your Coach (In a Book)

Mastering the Trickiest
Leadership, Business,
and Career Challenges
You Will Ever Face

Robert Hargrove

Michel Renaud

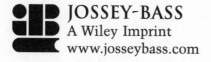

JOSSEY-BASS
A Wiley Imprint
www.josseybass.com

Published by Jossey-Bass
A Wiley Imprint
989 Market Street, San Francisco, CA 94103-1741   www.josseybass.com

Jossey-Bass books and products are available through most bookstores. To contact
Jossey-Bass directly call our Customer Care Department within the U.S. at 800-956-7739,
outside the U.S. at 317-572-3986, or fax 317-572-4002.

Jossey-Bass also publishes its books in a variety of electronic formats. Some content that
appears in print may not be available in electronic books.

Library of Congress Cataloging-in-Publication Data

Hargrove, Robert A., 1947-
  Your coach (in a book) : mastering the trickiest leadership, business, and career
challenges you will ever face / by Robert Hargrove, Michel Renaud.—1st ed.
       p. cm.
  Includes bibliographical references and index.
  ISBN 0-7879-7128-6 (alk. paper)
 1. Leadership. 2. Career development. 3. Mentoring. I. Renaud, Michel, 1956- II.
Title.
  HD57.7.H3653 2004
  658.4'09—dc22

                                                                    2004007627

Printed in the United States of America
FIRST EDITION
HB Printing   10 9 8 7 6 5 4 3 2 1

Contents

Elaine's working copy (handwritten)

Situation: How do you transform a climate of profound resignation into a climate of inspiration? What do you do with big aspirations and small resources? How do you shift from "running the business" to "creating the business"? *Let us be your thinking partner here.*

(handwritten margin note: Bk 33 pg. 40 pg. 43)

Situation: You declared your strategic intention and made great forward progress. Yet you have hit a wall and need to declare breakdowns to discover what is missing that will produce a breakthrough. *Your masterful coach will offer you a powerful assist.*

Situation: It was a terrific vision statement you came up with at the big meeting, but today it is just another good idea gone up in smoke. You keep asking yourself what's missing that will have impact. *Your masterful coach has a great leadership tool to offer you.*

Donna

Situation: The ways of being and thinking, the attitudes that were the source of your success in the past, have now become the source of your limitations. You're unaware of this, and you are unaware that you are unaware. *Your masterful coach will rip the blinders off.*

Situation: You have declared an impossible future and taken on a powerful business challenge, but sense you now need to take on an equally powerful leadership challenge that will require relentless coaching and feedback. *If you are ready develop faster, fasten your seat belt and let's go.*

Situation: You spent three months working on your Source Document as if you were writing your enterprise's version of the U.S. Constitution. You put out your vision, teachable points of view, and key priorities at town hall meetings with a bang, but what has come back is more like a whimper. *We'll show you how to get what you are committed to "over the line" so that it exists independent of you.*

Situation: You see an opportunity to make a difference and have jumped into action. It seems that each step you take creates a widening arc of support and opposi-tion. You know you have to deal with the opposition, but as you see it, playing politics is beneath you. *Get over it. To reach your goals you need to master the political chessboard.*

Situation: You've discovered that leaders get things done in three ways when they are not in charge: charisma, force of argument or pressure, and coalition building. What is the best way forward for you? *Here's a great mentoring tale.*

Situation: You are beginning to wake up to the fact that you cannot create an Impossible Future with a team of chronic C players. You'd give anything for a team of A players, if only it were possible. *Now it is!*

Situation: Your increasing inability to control your agenda has left you resigned and frustrated. You are spending way too much time reacting to the day-to-day demands of managing the business. You are wondering how you will ever be able to spend more time on activi-ties that will truly make a difference. *Here are the hidden keys.*

Situation: You have a big meeting coming up that is like a championship game for your business. You want your preparation for the meeting to match the opportunity and to come home with a big win. *Learn how to get the edge.*

Situation: You see others are getting ahead faster than you and can't figure out why. Perhaps their secret is not that they have more talent but that they have more ambition. *Your masterful coach will enable you to set your ambition free.*

Preface

Our Leadership Manifesto— *Better Leaders, Better World*

We aim to change the world with this Leadership Manifesto. Our purpose is to inspire, empower, and enable people who have the aspiration to become leaders to make a difference in their world. Our intention is to sound the tone for *"Better Leaders, Better World."* We believe that leaders in business, government, health care, education, and other organizations who hear this tone and respond by taking a stand for leadership development will meet with unparalleled success. We believe that those who are indifferent to the tone will meet with mixed fortunes at best. And we believe that those who do not hear the tone, like so many fallen CEOs, may be crushed by it.

We are committed to the proposition "Better Leaders, Better World." Just think for a moment what the implications of this statement might be in your world. In every nation, government, business, or public service institution, a critical few extraordinary leaders take a stand and make a difference. At the same time, there are a lot of very ordinary people who never stand for anything except more of the same. What if you could increase the number of those critical few leaders, if only by a small margin? It was the quest to develop extraordinary leaders that eventually led us to coaching people for leadership and business breakthroughs and that in turn led to many of the lessons in *Your Coach (In a Book)*.

Sounding the tone for leadership development is the most high-leverage thing any executive can do. Imagine the impact that multiplying the critical few extraordinary leaders would have on any nexus issue like conflict in the Middle East, hunger and starvation in Africa, or the health care system in the United States. Imagine the impact that it would have on transforming a business into an inspired, high-performing organization from a "me too" competitor with a climate of resignation. The persistence of pressing issues on a global, national, or business level is a flag for the fact that leadership is often missing. If we can acknowledge that leadership is missing and see it as an opportunity rather than a threat, we can begin to call forth the extraordinary leadership that is needed and wanted.

Why leadership development is more important than ever before in history. We wrote this Manifesto with a view toward creating a powerful new cultural clearing for leadership development in business, government, healthcare, education, science, the arts, and other organizations. Today this is more important than ever before; indeed, it may be a matter of CEO survival. In 2001, a record 555 CEO departures from Global 2000 firms were attributed to performance. The population of "key leader age" individuals will drop by 15 percent between 2000 and 2015, and those companies that don't develop leaders now may be priced out of the market. The financial consequences of selecting and developing one person in a role rather than another may be 100 to 150 percent. And finally, the challenge of managing corporations on a global basis in the midst of demographic shifts, joint ventures, and disruptive technologies will increasingly require extraordinary leaders.

Create a Powerful Leadership Pipeline That Gives Your Organization an Advantage

> Developing leaders is more important than developing a strategy.
> —Jack Welch

Today almost every major enterprise has a strategic planning book more than a hundred pages long. Yet few companies devote even one page of that book to developing leaders. Furthermore, research presented in the book *Leading the Way,* by Robert Gandossy and Marc Effron, shows that companies whose CEOs are involved in leadership processes delivered a three-year total return to shareholders (TRS) of 22 percent rather than a TRS of minus 4 percent where they were not involved.[1] Research shows that the vast majority of CEOs spend less than 10 percent of their time on leadership development.

> *It's imperative to make the business strategy and*
> *leadership strategy link.*

There are notable exceptions, and they are to be found in the top-performing companies. CEO Jeff Immelt of General Electric, Larry Bossidy of AlliedSignal, Claude Pepper of Procter & Gamble, and Roger Enrico of PepsiCo are noted for spending 25 percent to 50 percent of their time on leadership development. Why? These leaders make the business strategy and people strategy link. They have a maniacal focus on talent—getting the right people in the right job and never settling for less. They sponsor leadership programs that link leadership breakthroughs and business breakthroughs and consciously and intentionally nurture a coaching environment that allows these to be reached. They create world-class people processes that are fully integrated and focus on selection, development, retention, and succession.

How Do You Take Ordinary People and Develop Them as Extraordinary Leaders?

> *Leaders develop by creating futures, not filling gaps;*
> *through experiences, not abstract training programs.*

We believe that the prevailing paradigm of leadership development is bankrupt. It is as wrong-headed as the paradigm of medical science before Louis Pasteur. Leadership development typically consists of marching hundreds of people off to abstract training programs. There participants are greeted by talking heads who teach leadership behaviors, are encouraged to calculate their leadership gaps using 360-degree feedback computerized tick sheets, and are asked to participate in contrived classroom exercises to develop new skills and attitudes.

Our view is that despite hundreds of books and articles written, despite millions spent on research, despite thousands of three-day training programs presented, and despite universal acceptance, there is little evidence that the prevailing paradigm of leadership development works. Why not? It is based on wrong-headed assumptions, and if you get the assumptions wrong, everything else will be wrong too.

The Prevailing Paradigm of Leadership Development Is Wrong-Headed

The Prevailing Paradigm	*The New Paradigm*
• Leadership development is the charge of HR or OD people	• Leaders developing other leaders, starting with the CEO
• Leadership development is for the masses	• Leadership development starts with the critical few
• Leaders develop in the process of identifying and filling competency gaps	• Leaders develop in the process of taking a stand to make a difference and producing extraordinary results
• Leadership development happens in abstract training programs within limited time frames	• Leadership development happens by coaching people in specific situations in real time (twelve to eighteen months)
• Leadership skills and attitudes are a matter of tips and techniques	• Leadership skills are a matter of having something at stake, a sense of urgency, practice and study

A New Paradigm for Leadership Development

We would like you to re-imagine a bold new paradigm of leadership development that is based on a set of assumptions that are as different from the prevailing ones as night and day! Let's build out the new paradigm of leadership develop that gets right to the heart of our Leadership Manifesto.

> *Companies where the CEO is really involved in leadership development delivered a total return to shareholders of 22 percent over three years, versus minus 4 percent.*

New Paradigm #1. CEO and top executive spend 25 to 50 percent of their time in leadership development. The CEO is directly involved in leadership development in those companies that produce a graduating class of CEOs for other firms, as well as leadership bench strength. The most famous example is Jack Welch of General Electric, who said he spent 50 percent of his time on leadership development. He developed his successor, Jeff Immelt, Larry Bossidy of AlliedSignal, James McNerney of 3M, and Robert Nardelli of Home Depot. CEOs need to own leadership development, not automatically defer it to others. They must think of themselves as the top HR person in the company. They see leadership development and performance as totally integrated with performing, not a separate activity.

> *The impact of taking the small handful of extraordinary leaders in your company and doubling their number could be damn near immense.*

New Paradigm #2. Start with a critical few to spearhead a breakthrough in leadership development. At Masterful Coaching we get great results from our leadership coaching work, but much of the credit is due to starting with a few great people who have the aspiration to be great leaders. Coaching even one or two critical leaders to develop often leads to the development of leaders at all levels. For instance, people often start our executive coaching and take a stand for an extraordinary future for themselves and their company. They then often decide to work with one of our coaches and their team in an action-coaching program where each individual commits to a significant business breakthrough in service of that extraordinary future. Participants of the program are asked to coach two or three other people who report to them, producing a snowball effect.

> *Leadership is not a list of characteristics and traits but*
> *a matter of accomplishment.*

New Paradigm #3. Extraordinary leaders develop in the process of producing extraordinary results. We are often asked to give our opinion about leadership development programs by sincere, well-intentioned HR people. These programs are usually based on the prevailing paradigm of leadership development—studying characteristics and traits, filling competency gaps, and classroom exercises. Our typical response is, "A lot of the design elements of your program are great. However, the first question to ask when designing a leadership development program is, *What is the bow of the boat?* Our belief is that the bow of the boat in any leadership program is achieving a business breakthrough. Rather than asking, *How do you need to develop as a leader?* ask, *What is a significant business challenge you would like to achieve?* This often leads to a corresponding leadership breakthrough as people reach beyond themselves to achieve it."

> *The power of coaching is that it is focused on the*
> *individual's leadership and business breakthrough;*
> *it is situation specific and happens in real time.*

New Paradigm #4. Bring in coaching; retire training and the whole damn training department. Think about Tiger Woods winning the Masters and then working with coach Butch Harmon for an entire year, marching down every fairway in every tournament on the quest to win the Grand Slam (four majors). Picture them practicing for hours on end after each round the specific mindset and skills they will need to win the PGA Championship, the U.S. Open, and the British Open. Now imagine the average golf hacker, say, you or me, taking three sessions at the driving range, or a week at golf camp: we'd wind up with information anxiety, not tournament-winning skill. This metaphor shows the difference between coaching people to achieve leadership and business breakthroughs over the course of the year in real time and your typical three-day training program. This approach makes intuitive sense to almost every executive we speak to, yet most training managers just don't get it.

_____

> *To gain a new skill—golf, skiing, and so on—learn a little, practice a little, learn a little, and practice a little more.*

_____

New Paradigm #5. People learn new skills when they are faced with an immediate challenge and alternate between practice and performance. For example, one leader I coached, Greg, wanted to create an inspired organization. He created a Source Document that contained his vision and values. I then gave Greg some pointers on how to communicate his Source Document so that people were inspired by it. The feedback Greg got after a few town hall meetings showed that, while people liked Greg's ideas, he showed up as a bit cool and intense. I then coached Greg on calling himself forth as warm and engaging, and the feedback reflected he made huge progress. Again, this leadership transformation took place by intervening in the situation over time.

What to Do with the Leadership Manifesto: Better Leaders, Better World

Again, our purpose here is to sound the tone for leadership development and put it at the top of every enterprise's agenda, public and private. We also aim at smashing the prevailing paradigm of leadership development based on abstract training programs and creating a powerful new paradigm of leadership development based on the notion that extraordinary leaders develop in the process of producing extraordinary results. The idea here is to generate a new conversation about leadership development that is based on the premise that soft leadership skills produce hard results. If you find yourself aligned with the ideas presented here and want to be part of the future of leadership in the twenty-first century, please consider the following ways of participating:

- Send us e-mail and give us your views on the Leadership Manifesto—whether you agree or disagree with it. Robert. Hargrove@MasterfulCoaching.com.

- Send the Leadership Manifesto to leaders you admire and respect, requesting their written comment. We would like to get the written endorsement to attach to the Manifesto itself.
- Generate a conversation by sending the Leadership Manifesto to everyone on your e-mail distribution list and asking, "What do you think?" When you ask people this question, they get involved.
- Invite people to a brown bag lunch meeting where you will discuss the Leadership Manifesto. Ask people what they like about it, as well as for suggestions to build on it.
- Take a stand for leadership development in your organization. If you need help in bringing a leadership development forward or in designing one, please call us for a free consultation.

April 2004   *Robert Hargrove*
                                          Brookline, Massachusetts

                                          Michel Renaud
                                          Montreal, Quebec

Democratizing Coaching

This book came about as result of coaching executives to master some of the trickiest career, leadership, and business challenges any human being ever faced.

The coaching we do usually involves working with top executives of major corporations, government agencies, and other institutions on a one-to-one basis. We also do a team-based action coaching program with leaders at all levels. The combination of the executive coaching and team coaching represents a powerful force for achieving breakthrough results and breakthroughs for people.

Yet both of these programs take at least a year and cost sometimes astronomical fees. In a discussion with Susan Williams, executive editor at Jossey-Bass, we began to explore more deeply the notion of democratizing this work to make coaching available to leaders and high-impact players at all levels, at a fraction of the time and cost.

The idea developed to provide the nuggets of wisdom that we have mined from thousands of hours of coaching conversations with leaders at all levels, golden nuggets that have accumulated, one conversation at a time, in coaching people to reach their most important goals, resolve their most pivotal issues, and make their most crucial decisions.

The golden nuggets you will find here are the product of thousands of hours of extraordinary coaching conversations with leaders at all levels.

Why not provide an opportunity to be a fly on the wall, a privileged observer to conversations that address some of the most perplexing issues and dilemmas that leaders and managers face as they strive to maintain a competitive edge in a changing world? Imagine yourself fiercely engaged with your coach as you hear about a leader going from point A to point B, not just by creating a simple and obvious plan but also by mastering the corporate chessboard.

Imagine reading stories about extraordinary coaching conversations with leaders who have faced issues and problems just like yours—conversations that led to simple, powerful, but nonobvious solutions. Imagine the eye opening insights and new openings for possibility and action that could be triggered in you as you read with your own commitments at stake . . . your own red-hot issues!

We Wrote This Book with You in Mind

It's fascinating and intriguing to us that, although the leaders we work with come from very different kinds of organizations, they are often very similar in many respects. A chief executive in New York City faces the same leadership and business challenges as one in London, Paris, or Tokyo, even though they come from totally different industries. A midlevel manager who has a sincere intention to make a difference is as likely to wind up feeling thwarted by tyrants, walls, and organizational absurdities in high-tech, finance, or textiles. An emerging leader, a female executive, or a human resource guy is likely to face the same issues in any enterprise. We wrote this book with you in mind:

- Executives who want to build an inspired high-performing organization rather than a frustrating and infuriating low-performing one.
- Leaders at all levels who have an idea that could make a difference, but who have no idea how to master the corporate (enterprise) chessboard or human puzzle.
- Managers who are racking their brains for ways to achieve profitable growth on a sustainable basis and who may be in denial about their current business model.
- Women who are stuck on some ladder despite being better suited to leadership roles than many of the men around them.

- High-flyers who are hiding their burning ambition for fear of being labeled too ambitious.
- Leadership development professionals who are looking for a better way to develop leaders.
- Anyone who is sick and tired of feeling like a cubicle slave in an office that is ergonomically correct but mind-numbingly dull.

We Would Like to Engage You in an Extraordinary Conversation

As noted in Robert's first book, *Masterful Coaching*, "Coaching happens in conversations." Coaching conversations have a special place in our culture. They are not mere exchanges of opinion, nor are they conversations about predictable goals and obvious plans, and they are not conversations where you indulge yourself in gossip or rumor. They are conversations in which you talk about the opportunity in coaching. They are conversations where you are both challenged and supported to reach your highest goals and aspirations. They are conversations where you reinvent your organization, recognizing that to do so, you have to reinvent yourself first.

What do we mean by *challenge?* We often start by asking people to make declarations about the future they want to create, as well as the past they want to free themselves from. For example:

> I am no longer going to be swept along by history. Whatever I can imagine about who I can be and what I can do, I can accomplish, I can bring to pass. I am no longer a cubicle slave in a faceless bureaucracy who passively accepts the status quo. I am a revolutionary who brings about irreversible change. I am no longer a passive grunt or foot soldier in the long march of progress. I am an activist whose motto is: Never blame, never complain, do something!

What do we mean by *support?* We have written this book with one intention in mind—to cause your success. As we tell our coaching clients, "We start by standing in your greatness and giving you coaching and feedback in that context, never reducing our listening for you even when you fall from it." We know that you, the reader, are committed to being the kind of leader (player) who makes a difference, who has an impact, who is effective, and we join with you in that commitment. The focus of this book is not on what is wrong with you, it is on providing what is missing that will produce a breakthrough in reaching your goals.

We are speaking of leadership lessons that are powerful, profound, and practical and that apply to most people—and, in this case, more specifically to you. If you have ever felt frustrated in your attempt to demonstrate extraordinary leadership, or thwarted in producing extraordinary results in the very human and often imperfect environment of today's corporation, or caught in the conundrum of how to advance your career, you will find something of immense value for yourself here. All you need to do is read this book with a sincere commitment to reaching your goals and priorities, together with a willingness to be coached.

Perhaps you are saying to yourself, "Yes that's me, and I am dealing with some or all of the issues you're talking about, but what am I going to get out of reading *Your Coach (In a Book)* that will help? How is the book going to work?" If that is the case, we would like to ask you to use a little imagination. Imagine yourself picking up *Your Coach (In a Book)* puzzled about whether your job is really suited to your talents and gifts, struggling to get a result or to initiate change, and—wham!—find the championship-level coaching you need to succeed—the knockout insights you need to compete.

The Structure of *Your Coach (In a Book)*

Think of this book as a network of coaching conversations made up like a symphony of major movements and then smaller notes. We have designed *Your Coach (In a Book)* around three major sections:

Part One. Your Extraordinary Business Challenge

Part Two. Your Extraordinary Leadership Challenge

Part Three. Your Extraordinary Career Challenge

You will find an introduction to each of these sections that provides a frame of reference to begin thinking about that challenge. Taken as a whole, the sections are part of an integrated coaching process. For example, we generally start a coaching relationship by asking people what their business challenge is, then what leadership challenges they will face in achieving it. The chapters within each major section address a situation that you are likely to run into that presents the sort of puzzles, dilemmas, and conundrums involved in the chapter's topic. We then provide a "teachable point of view" that allows you to see things differently, followed by a "template for action" that allows you to act differently.

A Walk Through the Coaching Process

Let's take a look at the whole coaching process. Here is the sort of material we would cover if we were sitting together, along with some of the rationale behind it.

1. *What are your career, leadership, and business challenges?* Think about the tunnel at the entranceway to the Olympic Stadium, the foot of K2 or Mount Everest, or the stage wings of Carnegie Hall. There is something incredibly motivating to human beings about a real challenge that combines the aspiration to be all you can be by accomplishing the impossible with the feeling of aliveness that springs from knowing that possible success and failure are immediately at hand. As Connie Chung once said after many successful years of network TV when she was considering a whole new career, "I wanted to be challenged again. . . . I wanted to be scared again."[1] So tell us, what do you see as your biggest career, leadership, and business challenges?

2. *What's your situation?* The higher you set the challenge in your leadership and business challenge, the more you are likely to wind up in hairy situations. According to the *American Heritage Dictionary,* a *situation* is a critical, puzzling, problematic, or striking set of circumstances. *Your Coach (In a Book)* asks, "What is your situation right now? We're here to listen." For example, you might be faced with moving from vision to execution, dealing with a boss who is Dr. Jekyll one day and Mr. Hyde the next, getting a capital appropriation for your game-changing product idea in the face of scarce resources, building coalitions with supporters and opposers, or finding a new job based on your passion and talents. In the chapters, you'll find situations flagged with this icon:

3. *Here is a teachable point of view.* Our job as coaches is to listen so that we fully understand your situation, ask provocative questions that reveal the particular point of view, beliefs, or hidden assumptions that may be keeping you trapped, and provide you with a teachable point of view that allows you to see things differently and act differently. You'll find teachable points of view flagged with the following icon:

We would like you to listen to these teachable points of view in a certain way. Please don't listen from the point of view of "that's interesting," but rather, "here is something that could fundamentally alter who I am, what I do, and how I do it." For example: "I need to be a visionary, not just an administrator." Or, "This has gotten me to face the reality that I need to blow up my business model rather than continue tinkering with continuous improvement." Figure I.1 shows some teachable points of view.

4. *A template for action.* We typically say to our coaching clients at this point, "Now that you are seeing things differently, how are you going to act differently?" Perhaps you already have some ideas of your own that present openings for action in what was previously a stuck situation. At the same time, we would like to offer you some

Figure I.1. Examples of Teachable Points of View.

- Starting right now, tell yourself you are a revolutionary, an activist— not merely a pawn in their game or a foot soldier to history.
- As a leader, stand for something that addresses crying human needs and wants.
- A vision doesn't just happen; it needs to be "sourced."
- Learn to love politics if you want to get to the top of your profession or get something done in an organization.
- Balance passionate advocacy with inquiry.
- Don't blame anyone. Don't give up. Do something.
- Create a fascinating project that turns a boring job into a spine-tingling experience.

guiding ideas that will move you from pondering what to do to being ready to jump into action. The book is full of specific, small, high-leverage, actionable ideas you can put into practice right now, immediately, to make a big difference. In the text, templates for action will be flagged with this icon:

You will see that as we coach leaders in each of the dilemmas or problems that they face, we follow what we consider to be the *four steps of an extraordinary coaching conversation*. Figure I.2 shows these four steps. The intention is twofold: not only will you learn some of the secrets of masterful coaches, you will also learn something about how to have extraordinary coaching conversations, whether that's with the chief executive of your company, your peers, or your direct reports.

Okay, are you ready to get more power and velocity in developing as a leader and reaching your goals? Yes! Then buckle your seat belt and let's go.

Figure I.2. Four Steps of an Extraordinary Coaching Conversation.

1. *Draw people out.* Be a committed listener who is present to what's really on people's minds. Draw people out—not only to reveal issues and dilemmas, but also to explore underlying patterns of thinking and attitudes.

2. *Make an assessment.* Ask: How do you see things now? How do you need to see things differently? How are you thinking about this? How does your thinking need to change? What do you know? What do you need to learn?

3. *Offer a teachable point of view.* Provide basic human wisdom, guiding principles that have stood the test of time, and a powerful distinction that creates new openings for possibility and action. (For example: transformational versus transactional leadership.)

4. *Provide a template for action.* Make sure that you provide people with small, high-leverage ideas that they can immediately put into practice.

Chapter 1

What's the Opportunity in Coaching for You?

Coaching is for highly talented, successful people who seek an edge or advantage.

Chances are, since you have picked up this book, you are a talented person with a proven track record of success and a desire to create an extraordinary future for yourself and your organization. Is this mere flattery, an attempt to win you over? Absolutely not! It is a living, breathing fact of life.

We have learned through years of experience that it is highly talented, successful, ambitious people who are likely to recognize the opportunity in coaching. "You know, this might give me an edge in reaching my goals and aspirations," or "an advantage in changing the face of things."

People who see the opportunity in coaching are those who in sports have the profile of a champion, or who in the performing arts see their picture on billboards outside concert halls, or who in business show up in the pages of *Fortune* or *Fast Company*. They are the kind of people who want to take their game to a new level and to do so seek out the world's most masterful coaches.

People who are not so talented, successful, or ambitious tend to have lower goals and aspirations, avoid change, and adopt what we call the "Home Depot Do-It-Yourself" attitude. They keep trying to work the same old golf swing, get down the ski bumps with the same old ski techniques, grow their business by the same old business model, or get ahead by being a good soldier. They tend to be terminal intermediates at everything.

*You have a hunch perhaps that coaching can take you
to the next level of the game, or maybe change the game
you are playing altogether.*

Now that you have opened *Your Coach (In a Book)*, congratulations! You have just distinguished yourself from more than 95 percent of humanity. You are looking for a breakthrough in your career, your leadership ability, your business results, and more— and you relish the opportunity to get some great coaching, even if you don't exactly know who we are.

So what are you doing here? And what are we doing? Instead of thinking that you are opening a tome written by a couple of coaching gurus from far away, imagine that you are meeting us in your office, or a great restaurant, or a nearby Starbucks coffee shop for an extraordinary conversation.

You've got something on your mind that you would like to talk to us about—and we have something for you, too. All your life you may well have been told to genuflect before authority, to temper your personal dreams and aspirations, or to set predictable goals that could be achieved with a simple and obvious plan. Instead of being taught to think like a revolutionary, you were taught to think in terms of continuous improvement.

Let's sit down and talk . . . right there on those leather club chairs. What are you passionate about? What are your goals, aspirations?

What we are here to tell you is that it is time to widen your horizon of possibility—for yourself and your business, to unshackle your imagination from what you learned from the neighbors, from what they taught you in bean-counting school, and from what you absorbed in the white-collar towers of the typical Fortune 500 company.

Over the past two hundred years, millions of people came from the old country to the New World to create an impossible future for themselves, leaving caste and calling behind and succeeding beyond their wildest dreams. All great accomplishments started with a dream to accomplish something that looked impossible. This came to be known as the "American Way." Thomas Jefferson, James Madison, and Ben Franklin understood it. Andrew Carnegie,

Thomas Edison, and Horatio Alger understood it. Today, Andrew Grove, Jack Welch, and even Governor Arnold Schwarzenegger, a weightlifter and actor from Austria, all understand it.

Think back to 1950 and ask yourself, Who would have thought that by the year 2004 we would put a man on the moon, that the Soviet Union would be brought to its knees, that we would find a cure for the polio, or that 150,000,000 people would be communicating instantaneously via their own computers? Today, within just a few minutes or miles from you, people just like you are creating an Impossible Future, people who have thrown off caste and calling and dared to re-imagine themselves and their careers, people who are ready to take a stand that will make them stand out as leaders, people who are coming up with revolutionary ideas that will make their world—and yours—wobble on its axis.

Dare to Dream an Impossible Dream

What would you like to accomplish that looks impossible, but if it could be achieved, would change everything?

This book has one underlying theme—dare to dream about an Impossible Future and commit to making that the big game you play in life. For example, how about making the shift from "bag rat" (that is, "executive aid") to CEO of your company? From a good to a great leader? From a resigned to an inspired organization? From bankruptcy to profitable growth? From boring to fun! Coaching is about expanding your ability to take something that looks difficult or impossible and actually bring it to pass. It is not about getting coaching on something you already know how to do. Here is the picture frame:

- You don't need anyone's permission to begin.
- Everything is possible.
- Everything is likely.
- Every situation is transformable.
- There is always a path forward.

We say this because this is the context that we coach every leader, manager, human being that we work with, and we find it remarkably successful—much more successful than the alternatives: "My boss is a member of the ruling class around here and will never support this because it's too revolutionary." "It can't be done for a thousand and one reasons." "You can't transform people." "We're stuck and there is no path forward."

Our strength as coaches is to take people who have extraordinary talent and ability, but who often show up as ordinary under the circumstances found in most organizations, and help to free them before they reach their expiration date. One day while working on this book, we got an e-mail note that said, "If I didn't meet you guys, I might have wound up like the guy played by Jack Nicholson in *About Schmidt*." That piqued our curiosity enough that we went out and rented the movie.

The movie opens with Warren Schmidt, a sixty-six-year-old assistant vice president, sitting waiting for the clock to strike 5 o'clock on his last day of work at an Omaha insurance company. His colleagues' reflections of him at his retirement dinner spur Schmidt's own reflections. As he steps back and looks at his risk-averse life, he becomes increasingly distraught as he finds so little that has been meaningful.

When his wife unexpectedly dies, Schmidt decides to set off on a journey of self-discovery to explore his roots, going across Nebraska in a thirty-five-foot luxury motor home. One evening, he has a revelation and decides that the one thing he can do of importance is to talk his daughter out of marrying a guy he sees as an unworthy suitor. But his daughter fobs him off, and he participates in her wedding, playing the hail-fellow-well-met role and biting his tongue just as he has done all his life.

During this time, his "coach" or confidant turns out to be the six-year-old Tanzanian boy he is sponsoring for $22 per month through an outreach organization. His letters to the boy reflect all his suppressed dreams, unsaid thoughts, and withheld communications over the years. As he returns from his trip in the motor home, in his narration of the story Schmidt comes to the conclusion, "I never did one thing in my life to make a difference."

After watching the movie, we got into a conversation about what would have happened if Warren Schmidt had called us five, ten, or even twenty or more years earlier. We would have gone to meet him and talked to him about what mattered to him in his life, how he saw his dreams and aspirations, and how we felt about his present set of circumstances. Then standing in his greatness, we would say something like, "Schmidt, you strike us as a bright, talented guy, with a good character and personality. But you seem to have forfeited your dreams. Is this all there is for you?"

Then, after he muttered something half-inaudible, we'd say, "Schmidt, let us ask you some other questions. What would be an Impossible Future for you? Is it to be president of this company or division of it? Is it to create a truly inspired organization that combines compassion and edge? Is it to launch a new brand marketing campaign that takes your company to the top, based on the notion of, for example, 'Don't sell insurance, sell speed?' Is it to create an empowering management culture that enriches the lives of your employees?"

Schmidt's likely response? "Thank you, gentlemen. Those are truly inspirational thoughts . . . and I appreciate the sentiment. You're right! I would love to stand out as a leader and get promoted to president of the Omaha region, I would love to create an Impossible Future for the company, to transform this organization and maybe kick some butt. And I would love to make a difference, but I don't have the power."

Our likely response? "Fuhgeddaboudit! Can you imagine Thomas Jefferson, James Madison, George Washington saying, 'I don't have the power'? Can you imagine Abraham Lincoln, FDR, Jonas Salk saying, 'I don't have the power'? Can you imagine, Gandhi, Martin Luther King, Nelson Mandela saying, 'I don't have the power'?

"You get the power in the process of taking a stand for an Impossible Future for yourself and your organization, and then speaking, listening, and acting from your stand—which then results in other people standing with you. You get power in creating a structure for fulfillment that will deliver on the Impossible Future. And you get power from mastering the corporate chessboard, which we can show you how to do."

To which Schmidt might say, "Yes, but . . . I am used to setting goals that I know I can achieve and where there is a straightforward and obvious plan. It sounds like what you are talking about is something that may be impossible."

> *Coaching will give you access to a new kind of power,*
> *the power to make the impossible happen.*

To which our response would be, "Look, in the normal course of events, most people have the power to accomplish the predictable. What we're talking about with coaching is a new kind of power, the power to make the impossible happen. It starts with defining clear leadership, business, and career challenges for yourself, creating a structure for fulfillment as we just said, and then working shoulder to shoulder with us on these on a month-by-month, week-by-week basis."

Now let's assume Schmidt signed up for coaching. In the first month or so, standing in a commitment to his greatness as a leader, we would give him some powerful 360-degree feedback from the people closest to him and create a leadership development plan that would support him in standing up for his world-shaking ideas and acting more like a revolutionary or at least an activist than like a foot soldier in history's long march. Further, somewhere along the line we might have said, "Schmidt, to make a difference, you need to be authentic and to stop making things undiscussable. Here is my cell phone, go call your daughter (or wife, or whoever) and deliver the communication you have been withholding."

> *You may discover yourself miraculously emerging as*
> *an extraordinary leader in being coached to pursue*
> *extraordinary results.*

Then we would start working with him on creating a *Source Document*—a blueprint for the future—for his organization that tells people what really needs to be done and how to achieve it. Schmidt would soon start coaching his organization on the Source Document, touching people with his vision and timeless values while at the same time driving on results and having some significant bottom-line impact. Soon thereafter, you might read in the Omaha paper how Warren Schmidt, that once-gray manager, had risen to CEO and turned the company around.

This process of emergence is one that has happened countless times for our coaching clients who realized that there was more in their business life than they were currently experiencing, and they discovered the opportunity in coaching. It always reminds us of the way the sculptor Michelangelo worked on his great statue of David—"liberating the figure imprisoned in the marble," to use his own words—chipping away at the stone to reveal the masterpiece inside rather than trying to impose a design upon it. This is what we would like to do with each person we coach.

You Have the "What"—Here Is the "How"

We will inspire you to master the trickiest leadership, business, and career challenges you will ever face.

We said in the Introduction that this volume is designed to help you meet your own challenges. These challenges represent the "what." Let's take a moment here to give you the lay of the land with respect to the "how." Figure 1.1 outlines the how of coaching. Read the following sections with an eye to discovering the opportunity in coaching for you.

Declare an Impossible Future and Design a Structure for Fulfillment

Let's talk about your highest goals and aspirations, the world-shaking changes you want to bring about in your enterprise, and the things that are frustrating or even infuriating to you. We ask the

Figure 1.1. The Opportunity in Coaching for You: Our Promise.

1. We will coach you to declare an Impossible Future and design a structure for fulfillment that will help you reach it.
2. We will coach you to master the intricacies of the political chessboard, the vagaries and mysteries of the game.
3. We will help you to step back, give you perspectives, and see the big picture.
4. We will empower you to take creative and effective action.

people we coach, just as we are asking you, the reader: *What would be an impossible future for you? Do you have a burning personal ambition? What would be a "man on the moon" goal for you or your company? What's the one thing that you would like to change in your enterprise that, if you could pull it off, would change everything?*

Once we help people get clear about their highest goals and aspirations, we then work with them as coaches to create what we call a "structure for fulfillment" for realizing their goals. It is amazing how often we run into people who have created stretch goals and objectives that are based on unrealistic assumptions or where the actions do not add up to a realizable plan. Also, people tend to use more time-tested approaches and forget the importance of creativity and innovation.

Our approach at Masterful Coaching, which asks you to set some breakthrough goals for yourself as a leader and as a business, is distinct from the normal goal-setting process found in most companies. At the same time, we ask you to create a structure for fulfillment for those breakthrough goals, which is distinct from the normal planning process practiced in most organizations.

You will be hearing about this later, but to give you a quick overview, our approach involves setting some breakthrough goals, looking at where you are now with respect to them, and identifying what is missing that, if provided, will produce a breakthrough. Once we come up with what is missing, we ask people to create a route map and relationships map for getting there.

Master the Intricacies of the Corporate Chessboard

It's essential to master the political chessboard wherever you are, keeping in mind that what is frustrating and infuriating for some is an exciting human puzzle for others.

It was said of Lorenzo de Medici, grand master of Florence in Renaissance Italy, that he would sit down to dinner at his court with one hundred agendas and get up from dinner with each of these agendas accomplished. Medici was a great chess player. The dictionary defines chess as a royal game of strategy in which one tries to master one's opponent through skill and artistry. When we (the authors) play chess, we are often not very brilliant at all and, in fact, Michel's twelve-year-old son, Etienne, can easily clean the board with either of us in just a few powerful moves.

Part of the reason is that we tend to see the chessboard as a big enterprise controlled by kings and queens, where rooks and bishops can move diagonally or horizontally across the chessboard and pick us off at will. This causes us to play the game of chess not so as to maximize winning but rather to avoid losing. Thus we make one cautious move at a time.

Most of us push pawns on the corporate chessboard; we make one move at a time, naively hoping to get to the other side of the board and be crowned.

One of the things we like about chess is that a mere pawn can be transformed into royalty, and so we tend to push pawns across the board, one move at a time, with this single goal in mind, hoping to make progress, paying scant attention to anything else. Now the difference between pawn pushers like us and grand masters is that grand masters see the board from many different angles. It's almost as if they are playing on three to four chessboards at once.

If you have ever watched a grand master at work, you will see that such players take into account not just the individual pieces and all the complexity of their interactions but also the changing openings for possibilities and the constraints and the underlying patterns and connections. They grasp the game's evolving structure, anticipating opportunities to advance, and search for dangerous variables in the wide array of forces, grasping the mysteries and contingencies of the game.

Coaching can transform you from a pawn pusher on the corporate chessboard to a grand master.

What does this have to do with coaching, you might be asking yourself. What a masterful coach does is interact with you in such a way that transforms you from a pawn pusher to a grand master (masterful leader or high-impact player). The coach works with you to discover and express your personal and organizational aspirations, to map the chessboard, and to craft a master strategy necessary to succeed in your organization with colleagues amid change, complexity, and competition.

The following might help you think in terms of what you need to do to master the corporate chessboard:

• What are your most important personal and organizational goals and aspirations, the ones that are truly motivating you?
• Who are all the key pieces on the corporate chessboard—the players that you need to strategically influence?
• How can you engage both power wielders and power seekers in conversations where you listen loudly for what their positions are and where their interests lie?
• When you have clarity on the first three questions, ask yourself, How can I get where I am going by helping them get where they are going? See if you can come up with creative solutions.
• What contingency plans can you develop in case your idea doesn't fly?

Step Back and See the Big Picture

> *Most people we coach at some point lose all their perspective. They can't see the forest or the trees. They are stuck looking at the knot in the tree.*

In the fifth century, Sun-tzu, the Chinese political and military strategist who wrote *The Art of War,* said essentially that during an engagement, a leader should not be in the heat of the conflict but a small distance apart, else his perceptions may be distorted and he will misjudge the situation as a whole. We have found with the people that we coach that once they set clear goals and aspirations and a path forward and begin to take action, they may get so embroiled in day-to-day issues and problems that they cannot see the forest for the trees.

They might lose sight of the goals and aspirations they are most passionate about and become a victim of the calendar. Or they may get so hung up in their relationship with their boss that they stop being focused on what they want to create. Or they might get entangled in turf wars and political battles with colleagues about the change initiatives they want to bring about. Sometimes it's worse; they may wind up staring at one small knot and not even see a tree at all. What we do is help people step back and see the big picture. We focus on giving people an alternative view, one that is more accurate, insightful, and empowering.

Robert encountered a vivid example of this when coaching Ron Rosette, a regional vice president of a Fortune 500 firm, who was incredibly passionate about his vision and very driven. The problem was that he often pushed himself to the point of exhaustion and then started to take even the slightest criticism personally. Ron had put together a great strategy presentation for the CEO, seeking capital investment for his group. The CEO said that, although the substance of his presentation was along the right lines, he didn't like the style of Ron's presentation; it didn't energize anyone and was too detailed.

However, he made the mistake of telling Ron his criticism publicly. Ron called me during the break so embarrassed and upset that he was ready to quit his job on the spot. "Ron," I said, "as far as the affront to your leadership style, get some rest and get over it. On the substance side, you got 80 percent of what you wanted in that presentation. Go back and get the other 20 percent tomorrow." I was able to return Ron to what it was that he wanted to create and he went back into the meeting cracking a few jokes. I also urged him to take a vacation in the next couple of months.

Take Inventive and Effective Action

We've got to take our hats off to the leaders we coach because for the most part they are extraordinary human beings. They are usually so smart and knowledgeable about their business that they would stand out in any crowd, so tough and determined to reach their goals that they often work long hours for months on end, and so compassionate that they bend over backward to be fair.

And yet despite all of these superlatives, there often comes a point between formulating an Impossible Future and realizing it that these people become absolutely stuck and have no ideas as to the path forward. It is at this point that they call us up and bitch and moan for a while and then ask, "What should I do? What action should I take at this point?"

Frankly, we often don't have an easy or obvious answer. Imagine what you would say to Jack Welch after working on the GE Honeywell merger for over a year and being told by an official of the European Union, "No dice; go home, Mr. Welch." Imagine what you would say to Martha Stewart after she was indicted for securities fraud. Imagine what you would say to George W. Bush about how to find a noble way out of the quagmire of Iraq.

The situations that our coaching clients are in often involve changing times, enormous complexity, and competitive challenges. What we do is follow a process that you can follow by appointing a thinking partner in your own home or workplace.

- We assert that there is always a path forward, no matter how stuck things appear to be at the moment.
- We listen long enough to both empathize and make sure we understand the person's situation. We listen for goals and intentions and the person's strategies for realizing them.
- We ask some provocative questions that allow us to surface, challenge, and alter assumptions that could be resulting in the feeling of being stuck.
- Next we brainstorm alternative possibilities to the current course of action. (There are always more openings for action in the situation than the person is aware of.)
- We try to get three to six new alternatives on the table and ask the person to choose one or two that make sense. Then we suggest jumping into action to test which one of these approaches will work.

The Opportunity in Coaching for You

Before you engage in a coaching relationship with us, it is important for you to see the opportunity in coaching for you. One of the first things to consider is whether or not you have set high goals and aspirations that cause you to stretch your definition of yourself and your business, and thereby are likely to look at coaching as an opportunity or gift. If your goals are too low or if you don't have enough at stake in them, you may not see coaching as an opportunity at all.

Second, you may have high goals but may be frustrated or infuriated in the process of reaching them because you have not yet figured out how to master the political chessboard. If so, you'll have some burning questions on your mind and no idea how to answer them. For example:

- How do I keep from letting my temper get the best of me at the next big meeting and focus on making a great presentation instead of going in there wanting to strangle my boss?
- How do I get exposure to power wielders in this organization or others that could take my career to new heights?
- How do I build a coalition before the City Board of Zoning that speaks to three different special interest groups?

Third, if you are honest, you—like other leaders and managers today—are probably facing a number of problems, situations, or events where you could benefit from a coach, mentor, or thinking partner. Just take a look at the table of contents and see which topics jump out at you as something that you are dealing with. And ask yourself, What are the problems, issues, dilemmas that I am facing and what is the opportunity in coaching for me?

If you recognize that you have at stake your future and the future of your organization, are you willing to take a stand to create an extraordinary career for yourself and not settle for less? Are you willing to commit yourself to being an extraordinary leader and producing extraordinary results? Are you ready for a breakthrough in effectiveness?

If you are, you will find that we (the authors) will be like the wind at your back, supporting you 100 percent in everything we say in these pages and beyond them. In fact, you can even test that for being something more that hot air by sending us an e-mail note describing your goals, issues, problems, and so forth. We will do our best to provide an answer to your questions or a word of advice.

We wrote *Your Coach (In a Book)* with a particular commitment to you. We wrote it with a passion to save you time and make you rich in the insights needed to gain power and velocity in reaching your personal and organizational goals. We wrote it to help you gain the insights to crack open the problems, puzzles, and dilemmas that have been confounding you. We wrote it to make sure you receive the championship-level coaching you need to be super-successful.

We would like you to come to *Your Coach (In a Book)* with a particular commitment as well. We ask you to come to this book with a commitment to suspend any notion that you are a super-successful person who can do it yourself and to surrender to the idea of being coached for a while. We ask you to come to this book from a commitment to empower us as your coaches by being a committed listener and taking on the teachable points of view offered here. And we ask you to come from a commitment to taking these ideas and putting them into action. If you are willing to do that, then a great deal can be accomplished here.

Getting the Most Out of *Your Coach (In a Book)*

Before we begin our journey together, let us offer you ten things that we believe will help you make this book work for you.

- Write down your organization, business, leadership, and career challenges—and repeat the process several times within the next month to improve them, making sure they are something that will stretch your mind and skills.
- Compose a request for coaching. Write down your coaching objectives: goals you are struggling with, issues and dilemmas you need resolved.
- Read *Your Coach (In a Book)* with gusto. Dog-ear favorite pages; shamelessly underline valuable passages or even rip them out.
- Take the teachable points of view here and try them on for size. For example, for the next three months focus on creating the business instead of on running the business.
- Take the templates for action we provide seriously. Get going! Right now! Immediately, and just do it!
- E-mail us with the subject line "Request for Help" at Robert. Hargrove@MasterfulCoaching.com or Michel.Renaud@ MasterfulCoaching.com.
- Create a "deputy coach" or "thinking partner" in your organization who can give you ongoing coaching and feedback, and get your first three to four meetings on the schedule.

- Buy a copy of *Your Coach (In a Book)* for your deputy coach, thinking partner, or team.
- Create "Coaching Circles" with people in your team. Meet every Monday morning for half an hour about a particularly relevant passage in the book.
- Keep asking yourself, Is the coaching relationship extraordinary or ordinary? If it's ordinary, what do I need to do to make it extraordinary?

Part One

Your Extraordinary Business Challenge

We have talked about the opportunity for you in coaching. This section is designed to engage you in a conversation about creating an extraordinary future for yourself and your organization based on your highest goals and aspirations. We ground this conversation by asking you to begin thinking about formulating an extraordinary business challenge that allows you to both create an inspired, high-performing organization and maintain profitable growth on a sustainable basis. The following chapters will deal with the issues likely to come up along the way.

Here's a story that illustrates envisioning an extraordinary future based on a leader's highest goals and aspirations. Jim Nokes, a scrappy executive vice president of ConocoPhillips Corporation, a big oil company, asked Robert to consider coaching him and offered to lay out his goals and priorities for the year. His goals involved being a top-quartile performer in the industry for return on capital employed as well as increased cash and earnings from every business unit. I said, "Jim, the goals look good, but what I want to know is, are you passionate about them?"

Jim got a call from his executive assistant, Josette (who sometimes acts like the manager of a championship fighter), and had to step out of the room for a moment. It was impossible to hear what happened in that conversation, but when he returned, his expression showed that he had entered into what Teddy Roosevelt called "the arena."[1]

"Robert, let's put aside these goals for a moment," he said. "What I really want to do is become CEO and chairman, and transform this company. That's something I can be passionate about." That made the penny drop. It was clear from Jim's declaration of his aspirations what the coaching relationship would be about, and that he had so much at stake that this would be a powerful partnership. Jim needed coaching to reach his ambitious goal, something not true of the previous goals that he had set for himself, as important as they might be. Robert and Jim spent some time talking about his transformational vision and values, as well as about the need to formulate some really extraordinary business challenges for his organization in service of these.

"Jim," Robert said next, "what kind of leadership challenges do you think you will be facing in reaching these goals and aspirations? Do you think this is going to require a radical shift in your leadership style or an incremental one?"

"It's going to require a radical shift," Jim replied. "I am going to have to move beyond the leadership style that uses carrots and sticks to motivate people, and that has made me successful today. I am going to have to be much more of a leader that captures people's minds and hearts in going for something big. As you said before, more of a transformational leader rather than a transactional one."

"Jim, here are the next steps. You spend some more time thinking about your extraordinary business challenges and we will do some 360-degree feedback to find out how you show up as a leader today, which will tell us about some of the leadership challenges you will be facing. It will also provide us with some valuable clues about how to master the corporate chessboard you happen to be on."

What Is an Extraordinary Future for You and Your Organization?

We've told this story for a reason, to get you to start thinking about an extraordinary future for yourself and your organization. Start by asking yourself if you have an ambitious aspiration for yourself—like being chief executive of your company, a business unit leader, or perhaps owner of your own new business. Then ask yourself if you have an equally ambitious aspiration for your company. For example, to create an inspired, high-performing organization that unleashes the human spirit and generates real action.

Can you express your aspiration for your company in terms of an inspiring vision that captures people's minds and hearts, or a set of empowering values that resonates with what really matters to people? In most organizations, powerful voices are always calling for optimizing "what is." Can you imagine yourself being a voice that maximizes "what could be"? Robert Shapiro, CEO of Monsanto, has the stated goal of "Feeding the World," based on the value of meeting basic human needs and wants. Not bad for an agriculture products company.

Now, moving from your transformational vision and values into the real world, do you have a strategic goal or intention that carves off competitive space, something that can become a corporate battle cry? Let's say you have a goal that is the twenty-first-century equivalent of *Man on the Moon by the End of the Decade* written up in the lobby of your building; do you have a structure for fulfillment that addresses the major building blocks to be put in place and obstacles to be overcome, as well as gets everyone in your organization committed and involved on a daily basis?

And finally, who do you need to be as a leader to achieve all this? In coaching people in various kinds of enterprises, we always tell them that, if their goals and aspirations for an extraordinary future don't cause them to have to step up and be extraordinary leaders, then they have not raised the bar high enough. So consider the following: What would you like to accomplish if only it were possible? What change would you like to initiate, if only it were achievable? What do you care so passionately about that it would be worth re-inventing your entire self?

Five Aspects of an Extraordinary Business Challenge

Taking into account everything we have said here, you now have the basis for thinking about how to formulate your extraordinary business challenge. Figure Part 1.1 shows five aspects of an extraordinary business challenge. Let's look at each one.

Stand for Something

Your extraordinary business challenge includes taking a stand for something that becomes the vision, climate, and spirit of the company. We are talking about taking a stand that both makes a difference

Figure Part 1.1. Five Aspects of an Extraordinary Business Challenge.

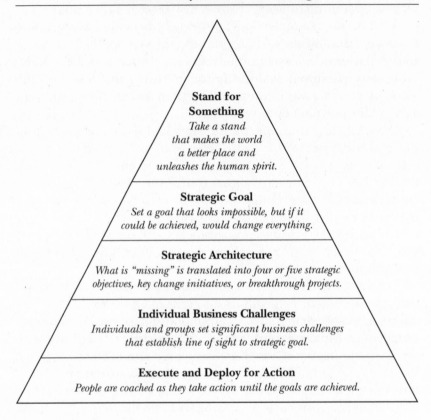

Stand for Something
Take a stand that makes the world a better place and unleashes the human spirit.

Strategic Goal
Set a goal that looks impossible, but if it could be achieved, would change everything.

Strategic Architecture
What is "missing" is translated into four or five strategic objectives, key change initiatives, or breakthrough projects.

Individual Business Challenges
Individuals and groups set significant business challenges that establish line of sight to strategic goal.

Execute and Deploy for Action
People are coached as they take action until the goals are achieved.

in the world by addressing real human needs and at the same time makes money for shareholders. Taking a stand like this not only gives everyone in your organization a big game to play, it unleashes the human spirit into action.

Around four o'clock one afternoon, William Campbell, a scientific researcher, took off his glasses and leaned back in his swivel chair wondering about the data from his experiment. In the process of testing a new compound to fight parasites in animals, he had an "aha" insight that the compound might be effective in fighting another parasite, one that causes blindness and itching in humans in such an agonizing way that some unfortunate victims have committed suicide.

Dr. Campbell might have just mentioned this to a colleague and gone home on the train. After all, potential customers for such a drug were not affluent North Americans or Europeans. They were tribal people in remote locations in Africa, India, and Australia who would have no money to spend. Undeterred by this, Dr. Campbell wrote a letter to the leadership of his firm, Merck and Company, passionately arguing for following through with this idea. Today, thirty million people a year receive Mectizan—the drug that came out of his "aha" experience—mostly free of charge.

George Merck created a context that became the vision, climate, spirit of his company and unleashed the human spirit into action.

As one observer noted, the most exceptional part of the story was that it wasn't an exception. George Merck II, the company's founder, set out to produce drugs that ended human suffering. He declared on the cover of *Time Magazine* in August 1952, "Medicine is for people, not for profits." This inspiring vision and the empowering values that went with it not only led to distributing Streptomycin to Japanese children after World War II but also to a powerful context at Merck that shapes, limits, and defines the way people think and interact on a day-in, day-out basis.

To be sure, George Merck was not just a fuzzyheaded altruist who wanted to save the world. He simply believed that the purpose of a corporation was to do something that made a difference in the world and, if that happened, it would attract talented people who would be inspired to bring their whole selves to work. Merck was also a hard-edged businessman who said, "If we remember this, the profits will never fail to appear." He sounded a tone that people could not forget, and Merck's profits have been extremely large by all industry standards. His example provides a counterpoint to chief executives whose fixation with Wall Street investors have in the long run not produced either profits or benefits to people.[2]

Create a Strategic Goal

Your strategic challenge needs to include a "man on the moon" type goal that captures people's imagination and becomes an omnipresent focus. It should take into account that the real objective of any enterprise is to achieve profitable growth on a sustainable basis. It must also include what strategy maven Gary Hamel calls "the quest for strategic resilience" or the capacity to reinvent your business, given that it must operate in a turbulent world where incumbency is worth less than ever and you are likely to hit the wall of diminishing returns.[3] This can only happen if you are first willing to reinvent yourself—to get past denial, arrogance, and nostalgia. Some examples: being #1 in market leadership, producing 10 percent growth and 20 percent earnings every year, coming up with a game-changer that alters the economic premise of your business or industry.

Your strategic challenge must become an enterprise battle cry, providing an opportunity to focus, energize, and even transform your organization.

John Young is Assistant Secretary of the Navy. His job is to research, develop, and acquire systems that enhance the Navy's warfare capability today and in the future. This means putting ships in the water, planes in the air, and, if necessary, well-equipped marines on the ground in the studied and predictable manner of his predecessors. Shortly after he was confirmed by the Senate, however, 9/11 happened and the world was turned upside down.

During the cold war, the Navy sent ships to counter the efforts of a known enemy—the Soviet Union—and to the same known geographic locations, whether in the Atlantic, Pacific, or Baltic Sea, to maintain the status quo and the balance of power. This allowed for a predictable schedule of shipbuilding, deployment, and maintenance. In a post–cold war, post–9/11 world, where the enemy is an unknown terrorist group whose location could be anywhere and everywhere, it has become important to develop a "surge" Navy that can deploy with much more intelligence, speed, and agility.

Secretary Young saw that 9/11 changed everything. The mission for the Navy was no longer "Beat the Russians," it was now "Strike anyone, anytime, anyplace."

This would require not just developing new strategic options based on getting better at past weaponry, but developing a whole different approach and creating the Navy of the future. This in turn would require transforming the thinking and attitudes of his 60,000-member organization and a sizable chunk of the military industrial complex.

Thus John Young began thinking in terms of a new Navy, saying that we risk emboldening our adversaries by assuming the battlefield of the past will look like the battlefield of the future. He began making speeches and working on a Source Document with me that built on the ideas of Secretary of Defense Rumsfeld: "Our enemies are transforming and we need to transform as well." He began thinking in terms of a different paradigm for the Navy based not on bulk but on converting bulk into intelligence. He began asking himself fundamental questions, like "What good is a submarine or a battle ship or even a joint strike fighter against an al Qaeda terrorist?" He realized that a walkie-talkie that is interoperable for the Army, Navy, Marines, and CIA could be more useful in a terrorist enclave than a unit of armored tanks.

Then he began to formulate a strategic challenge for the Navy based on winning the present war against terrorism and preparing now for future wars—wars notably different from those of the past century and even from the current conflict. His vision was based on developing a smaller fleet of surface ships, subs, and planes with revolutionary designs that would be extraordinarily effective at gathering intelligence in both peacetime and wartime about the enemy's whereabouts, allowing the Navy to engage the enemy through precision strikes and covert insertion of special operations forces.

To succeed with such a vision, Young and his counterparts (such as the Chief of Naval Operations) needed to develop a whole new range of strategic options, which in turn required making some tough trade-offs. For example, do you bring out the next generation of certain aircraft today or wait longer until a truly revolutionary technology can be developed? How do you get military defense contractors to produce revolutionary capabilities faster and ensure their earlier integration into the Navy? How do you get different services to collaborate on leveraging information technology and innovative, network-centric concepts to link up joint forces? Finally, where do you deploy scarce resources? Where can you cut costs? What programs do you cancel and who do you piss off?

To succeed with his transformational vision, he not only needed to get his message through, he also had to master the political chessboard of the military industrial complex with its many competing special interests. It involved creating allies and strategically influencing the uniformed Navy (many of whom were cold war warriors with a penchant for just getting more ships in the water and planes in the air) to think about how they could do more with less and in some cases with more intelligence, agility, and swiftness. It involved building coalitions with members of Congress, so as to increase support and diminish opposition, especially from those who might find a shipyard in their district closed. It meant cultivating relationships with the CEOs of Lockheed Martin, Northrop Grumman, Raytheon, and other suppliers with the intent of speeding up delivery times and reducing costs.

It wasn't all smooth sailing and there were real challenges in meeting some of the resource requirements. Secretary Young learned by doing—along with some coaching about how to create powerful relationships with people in power, as well as with thought leaders and opinion leaders. To his credit, John Young has the rare quality of being both strong on vision and strong on execution. He came up with some innovative ways to negotiate deals, developed some innovative products, and saved quite a bit of money doing so.

Design a Strategic Architecture to Produce a Breakthrough

Your extraordinary business challenge needs to include not just a strategic goal or intention but a strategic architecture that will sustain it through a series of immediate business challenges until it is realized. This involves taking the strategic intention and looking at where you are now with respect to it and determining what's missing that, if provided, can make a difference. What's missing is translated into four or five strategic objectives, key change initiatives, or breakthrough projects.

Marks & Spencer has been a leading British retailer for over 100 years and has an unrivaled reputation for selling high-quality products, as well as introducing hundreds of new and exciting products each year. Their mission is "making aspirational quality accessible to all." In their food business this translates into providing aspirational food in a way that connects with people's lifestyles and the increasing demand to experience authentic "foreign" food at home, making everyday eating special. They actually bend over backwards to deliver on their promise by employing a large team of people who scour the world to experience firsthand the excellence and authenticity of local food and then painstakingly translate that into products for their retail stores.

Stand in a Marks & Spencer store and contrast the scene in your mind to a supermarket in the United States and you will feel that you have stepped into a time machine and leapt years ahead. You won't see a big box store like Shaws or a glorified warehouse like Costco with aisles stacked with "air" bread, canned soup, and shrink-wrapped, three-pound packages of 70 percent fat-free hamburger. Instead, you will see a smartly designed store with invitingly packaged foods that are either ready to eat or heat, and that represent the ultimate in convenience—from fresh Nova Scotia scallops with herb butter to an authentic Indian fish curry or a fresh cream strawberry and champagne soufflé. Sandwiches, sushi, and prepared fruits, also in convenient packages, satisfy the customer on the move who desires good quality and tasty food.

Aspirational? Marks & Spencer caters to a wide range of audiences, including an increasingly upward-mobile, professional crowd with gourmet tastes, little spare time on their hands, but a desire for excellence. Taking each eating occasion and meeting the demands of this audience is a real skill, and Marks & Spencer have turned this into an art form. From their mouthwatering everyday dishes like Italian cannelloni, to a dinner party special such as duck a l'orange, or a Christmas feast of stuffed boned turkey with all the trimmings, you will feel as if you have been transported to the cucinas that surround the Roman steps, the restaurants of Paris, or a baronial hall in the English countryside.

Innovative and high quality? The company is devoted to making people's lives better. It was the first company in England, for example, to provide a fresh food offering on a mass scale at a time when the only way you could buy, for example, a chicken was either frozen or at the butchers with its head on. However, as time went on, Marks & Spencer began to lose its competitive edge in the marketplace as the one time "game-changer" and "game-grower" became just another "me too" competitor.

In the early 2000s, Marks & Spencer's profits were sagging, and growth was sluggish. The company was very much in the middle of a quest for resilience with a new chairman and chief executive and a new strategic challenge of growing the business dramatically, while restoring profitability and providing shareholder value. "In a sense," says our client Chris Head, "Marks & Spencer had become a victim of its own success." The competitors saw an opportunity to sell fresh foods at good margins and copied Marks & Spencer on a larger scale and importantly in more convenient locations—principally in the big out-of-town superstores. In so doing, competitors, such as Tesco and Wal-Mart ASDA, ate into the market share and in some sectors of the food markets became the leaders.

The leadership of Marks & Spencer decided to address this with a strategic goal that involved extending their reach to the customer and taking back market share. They then began looking at the strategic architecture of actually achieving this. The first piece of the strategic architecture involved a game-changing idea of adding 500,000 square feet of new stand-alone food space, which translates into about 150 new stores, with a new concept called Simply Food. These would not be conventional supermarket-type stores or convenience stores, but rather smaller grocery boutiques placed in convenient locations like rail stations to capture the high volume of passing traffic or in small towns where access to the Marks & Spencer main store meant traveling some distance to a city center with all the complications of parking and congestion. The idea was to put Marks & Spencer within 10 minutes traveling time of every customer in the United Kingdom.

This then led to another piece of the strategic architecture, an initiative called Project Diamond, led by Chris Head, which would in essence be the enabling tool to support the business growth and deliver success. Project Diamond would focus not only on the logistical aspects of servicing these stores but also on the buying, range planning, and forecasting elements essential to provide the customer with the right product where she wants it when she wants it. The aim was to be able to service this increasing number of stores without increasing the costs associated with such an ambitious expansion program.

Create Line of Sight to Each Individual on the Team

Once you have taken a stand for vision or values that unleashes the human spirit and declared a strategic goal and strategic architecture that tells you the major milestones, objectives, and key projects, the last step involves asking everyone in your group to come up with significant business challenges based on what really needs to be done. This is a way to bring hundreds of people into the big game as players, focusing the emotional energy of your organization.

The distinction "significant business challenge" was invented by an executive I coached, Greg Goff, president of ConocoPhillips International Downstream. Greg observed that, while people set goals every year, most of the goals were not linked to a clearly defined strategic intention, not really challenging, and not going to make any difference. He also observed that whether or not the goal was realized, in fact, often had more to do with the power of your brand, the richness of your assets, and what was happening in the business environment—in his business, the rise and fall of the price of oil and refining margins.

Greg came up with the idea of the significant business challenge to "change the game" of the goal-setting process with a view to creating an inspired, high-performing organization. He began by asking the following questions:

- What stretch goal have you set that is in service of our strategic intention?
- Is it a challenge?
- Will it make a difference?

It is amazing how powerful asking these questions can be.

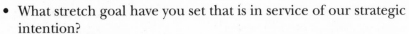

The problem with most goals people send to corporate headquarters is they are not a challenge, and they don't make any difference.

We adapted this line of questioning into a team-coaching program—Action Coaching—for key people in Greg's organization.

The purpose was both to help people formulate their significant business challenges and also to help them frame challenges in terms they could carry out. We added several more questions: Can you express it clearly and powerfully in emotionally compelling language? Do you experience a healthy level of excitement and anxiety about it? (We found that, if the statement didn't evoke a healthy level of excitement and anxiety, it was probably not a significant business challenge.)

Greg uses setting significant business challenges as a way to make sure people set stretch goals in the right direction and to hold them accountable for making a difference, and also as a metric for helping him decide who gets promoted and who doesn't. One day the managing director from the Swedish business unit office came to Greg and said, "I would like to put Stefan up for a promotion in our marketing department." He went on to say that Stefan had done a good job keeping their supply and trading business on an even keel.

Greg, who knew something about this manager said, "I will support your decision to promote him, if you can tell me one thing he has done to make a difference." The managing director reflected on this and then said, "I can't think of anything." Greg replied, "Tell him I expect him to make a difference in that new job and I will keep track of how he is doing in it." Whether your organization's leadership has defined an extraordinary future or a big game, asking people on your team to create a significant business challenge is a way to raise the bar for everyone in your organization.

> *Asking leaders at all levels to come up with a significant business challenge that leads to "wow" projects is not only a way to get people involved, it is a way to create and manage accountability.*

At the same time, if your organization has a declared strategic goal or intention, asking key leaders and their groups to create a significant business challenge that sustains that intention and that becomes an omnipresent focus is powerful, especially if people are coached in action to deliver.

Let's return to the Marks & Spencer example for a moment. As you will recall, the company had a strategic goal of growth. Part of the strategic architecture involved adding 500,000 square feet of stand-alone space (about 150 stores) through the Simply Food store format, along with Project Diamond to reinvent the supply chain to support that.

The Project Diamond teams came up with some innovative ideas for reinventing the supply chain and significant business challenges were created in each of the four main areas:

- "Display Management," which created a store-specific layout plan by using a new intuitive technology for in-store merchandising delivered on a weekly basis that would take advantage of range changes, special promotions, and so on.
- "Flowed Deliveries," which involved using information from display management and the forecasting system to provide the right quantities of food delivered to the stores at the right time so as to maintain freshness and eliminate waste and the need for staffers to double-handle excess amounts of stock. It also would allow the company to cater to the different store sizes in a more precise way.
- Automating range planning and store cataloguing, which allowed the company to make better use of customer information and lifestyle and plugged a gap in the way in which the business met customer needs more effectively. This in conjunction with more in-depth analysis of sales trends created a better base on which to predict likely future demand.
- Challenging the way people had traditionally done their jobs, which meant putting new diagnostic tools in the hands of people with the right expertise. It also meant letting go of some of the detail and trusting in automated processes to do the drudge-work for them.

The project team recognized that successfully delivering such a substantial enterprise change would require an approach that captured the imagination of the organization and engaged and generated proactive sponsorship. They participated in a team-based coaching program where they identified the business challenges, worked through the potential solutions, and developed a clear view of how to manage the change into the business. This approach and methodology enabled the team to easily identify its strengths and weaknesses, allowing it to seize the opportunities to deliver into the business.

Take Action

The final part of your extraordinary business challenge involves moving from grand visions and big challenges to action. The key to this is to create a leadership and management culture based on execution.

Larry Bossidy is one of the world's most acclaimed chief executives, a man with few peers who has a track record for delivering results. After a long, stellar career with General Electric, Larry Bossidy transformed AlliedSignal into one of the world's most admired companies and was named CEO of the year in 1998 by *Chief Executive* magazine. His accomplishments, such as thirty-one consecutive quarters of earnings-per-share growth of 13 percent or more, didn't just happen; they resulted from the consistent practice of the principle of execution—the art of getting things done.

Bossidy thinks that the most important job any leader has, once the (vision) strategic intention is clear, is execution with respect to the specific challenges that are involved in bringing it to pass. He feels strongly that the leader must be involved in executing, rather than leave this work to others. According to Bossidy, the heart of execution lies in linking the three core processes of any business— people, strategy, and operations—to result in a business based on intellectual honesty and realism. The most important by far, says Bossidy, is the people process: "Getting the right people in the right jobs." If you get the right people in place and develop them, those people will create the right strategies, and the drive for effective operations must follow.[4]

We have found at Masterful Coaching that many companies set aspirational goals, but they are often weak on creating a structure for fulfillment based on realistic assumptions and actions that add up to a probable result. They are also weak on executing.

We have designed a team-based Action Coaching program that addresses all this and is based on the premise that you can't manage people on goals, only on what they do. People get together as a team with a coach and their team leader once a month for a full day, declare leadership and business challenges, come up with a structure for fulfillment, and design inventive and effective actions to be taken in the next thirty days. They then work with the leader, the coach, and their colleagues (until the results start to add up) using the following protocol: What's happened? What's missing? What's next?

Coaching in this way consistently produces leadership breakthroughs, business breakthroughs, and team breakthroughs, while at the same time fostering a coaching environment where people stand for each other's success.

The Chapters in This Section

The chapters in this section of *Your Coach (In a Book)* are designed to give you clarity and power in dealing with the issues and problems you encounter in realizing your business challenge. First we will focus on articulating an Impossible Future for your organization—something that goes beyond what has made you successful in the past. Then you will learn a process for getting grounded in current reality and discovering what is missing that will make a difference. From there you will find out how to create a Source Document and create line of sight to the Impossible Future by getting leaders at all levels to create their own significant business challenges.

You will also discover how to take a business that is stuck in neutral with respect to top-line growth and both regenerate your core business and break the grip of denial to come up with innovative business concepts that create new wealth. You will be able to get the resources that you need from the powers that be when you forget about doing a presentation and instead engage people in a conversation and think about it as a negotiation. Finally, you will discover the power of shifting from a "me" point of view to a "you" point of view to create stellar customer service.

Here are some examples of the kinds of Extraordinary Business Challenges you can pursue:

- Ask each manager to generate 10 percent growth each year, with 20 percent return on equity. (GE Capital)
- Grow your business through a monster acquisition where you go from niche player to the biggest and best in your industry. (ConocoPhillips)

- Create a business concept innovation using the Internet that takes you out of the dry gulch of also-rans to a gusher of opportunity. (Amazon)
- Create an efficient business model and work to get the lowest breakeven costs. (Southwest Air—lowest cost per mile)
- Create an efficient business model with service embellishments without the lowest breakeven costs. (Midwest Express—best care in the air)
- Grow your business organically in retail: One more dollar or euro per customer. (ConocoPhillips, Jet Gas Stations, Germany)
- Declare that all business processes in manufacturing, marketing, and so forth should be running at Six Sigma quality—ninety-nine defects out of a million. (Motorola)
- Transform your supply chain into a competitive weapon. (Dell, FedEx)
- Turn procurement into a strategic advantage by partnering with suppliers. (Marks & Spencer)
- Create a list of profit boosters and pursue them—the law of increasing returns, competitor lock-out, customer lock-in, supply chain efficiency. (Dell Computer)
- Come up with one breakthrough product or service each year that results in 30 percent of your income. (3M)
- Create a digital dashboard with monthly metrics on key drivers of your business. Manage these key drivers rather than getting down in the weeds to watch every detail. (General Electric)

Chapter 2

Declare an Impossible Future

That Captures People's Imagination

 SITUATION: How do you transform a climate of profound resignation into a climate of inspiration? What do you do with big aspirations and small resources? How do you shift from "running the business" to "creating the business"? *Let us be your thinking partner here.*

Robert in a Coaching Conversation with an Oil Company Executive

I was sitting in the main salon of Richard Severance's forty-five-foot boat, *Dream Catcher,* in a marina on the Gulf Coast near Houston, Texas. The charismatic "Severance," as he calls himself, is president of Conoco North American Downstream. In my mind, he would be played by Tommy Lee Jones in the movie version of *Big Oil,* except that, unlike Tommy, Severance has only one arm; he is so adept with his hook he can cut a hangnail with a clipper.

"Hargrove," he said, looking at the remains of a crawfish soup lunch on my Bobby Jones sport shirt, "you're an insult to good clothes."

"Well, Severance, that's what you call eating with gusto; my compliments to the chef. But let's see if you are as good a leader as you are a chef." After a bit more good-humored repartee, I said, "Severance, in the ordinary course of events there are two kinds of leaders, those who take a stand for a vision of an Impossible Future and make things happen to bring it to pass, and those who take a stand for a predictable future and are thereby swept along by history. What kind of leader are you going to be?"

"Now just hold it right there!" he protested. "What's the point of going for a future that is impossible, when by definition, it's never going to happen?"

"Just a minute now," I replied, "if you look at history, whether in politics, business, or science, all great accomplishments—the building of the Panama Canal, the invention of the telephone, the first Ford Model T factory, the invasion of Normandy, or the creation of the Salk vaccine—looked impossible. The problem with most leaders and managers is that they tend to get lost in a sea of predictability."

"Well, there's a good reason for that," he retorted. "We have to meet our earnings forecasts for Wall Street. And to do that, we keep doing what we're good at, *buying, boiling, and selling oil.*"

"I think there is another reason why this happens that is just as important," I countered. "Most organizations have what I call a 'winning strategy.' Your winning strategy is the source of your success—but at a certain point, it becomes the source of your limitations. It's like a box that, once inside the box, you can't dream, think, or act outside of it."

This is what BCM's are doing. [handwritten margin note]

"I see what you are driving at," he said. "Instead of setting high goals, you set goals that you can achieve based on your winning strategy. Instead of thinking about what could be, you keep thinking in terms of what has been."

"Yes, and instead of coming up with game-changing ideas, you keep polishing up the existing assets through continuous improvement. Instead of welcoming innovative ideas, you suppress them and end up creating low morale in the company. That winning strategy will never take you to an Impossible Future, only to a probable future. Nor will it test the mettle of your organization."

"So how you break out of the box," he pondered, "and at the same time deliver on your results today?"

"Setting high goals is one way to expand beyond your winning strategy, because these goals cannot be realized within it," I said.

Severance talked about the possibility of creating an Impossible Future at his next executive team meeting—a three-day powwow he held every month. I said, "That's a lot of time to spend together as a group. Just what do you create at those meetings?" Severance's eyes opened wide in response, as if coming to a moment of true insight. "We don't create anything at those meetings," he said slowly. "We run the business."

"Perhaps the way out of the box of your winning strategy is to not only set some high goals for yourself, but also to begin to think in terms of 'creating the business' versus 'running the business.' Instead of seeing your business as limited to your current model— *buy, boil, and sell oil*—see your business as a capacity to create new wealth by staking out new areas of opportunity that represent getting different, as well as getting dramatically better at what you are already doing." *sales / day* [handwritten note]

In the following months, I coached Severance and his group to create an Impossible Future based on some BHAGs (big hairy outrageous goals) that were designed to transform a climate of resignation into a climate of possibility and opportunity and at the same take people beyond the increasingly dry well of "buy, boil, and sell oil" into a gusher of new opportunity. With that strategic challenge clear in our minds, the next step involved holding a CollabLab where we brought an extraordinary combination of people together to brainstorm on how to deliver on it.

The strategic architecture that came out of the CollabLab involved a business incubator for innovative business concepts, a leadership development program based on Masterful Coaching, a Six Sigma quality program, and an organizational renewal process.

In speech after speech, Severance preached his Impossible Future, creating the context of a truly inspired organization. Hundreds of leaders went to a whole new level through the application of both executive coaching and team-based coaching. Innovative business concepts were experimented with that had the potential to create new sources of wealth. Six Sigma quality resulted in dramatic efficiency improvements to the tune of $200 million while giving individuals at every level the experience that they could make a difference.

 TEACHABLE POINT OF VIEW: Leaders create an Impossible Future; administrators maintain the status quo.

> *Tell yourself, "Anything I can imagine is possible." Let your mind test the limits: "If only . . . , if only . . . , if only . . . ."*

If you wake up every day and go to work and ask yourself, "Is this all there is?" you are probably spending too little time creating an Impossible Future and too much time in the dull process of administering the status quo. Perhaps your epitaph would be something like this: "Made the budget twenty-seven times, shrunk the organization, and played the corporate politics pretty well." Now imagine a new epitaph: "[Your Name] accomplished the seemingly impossible feat of . . . and changed the world of [your industry] irreversibly and for the better, while enriching the whole organization."

> *Create your own 2004 version of a "man on the moon" goal for yourself and your enterprise.*

Declare an Impossible Future

By declaring an Impossible Future, you create a context that breaks the grip of profound resignation that plagues most organizations.

This will create opportunities for people to grow as they stretch their minds and skills in the pursuit of high goals. Instead of paying attention to what you can predict based on history or your organizational winning strategy, pay attention to what you can declare. Start by asking yourself the following questions: What would you like to accomplish, if only it were possible? What change would you like to bring about? (Pick something that looks impossible, but that—if it could be done—would change everything.) What do you passionately care about so much it would be worth reinventing your entire self?

Find people and businesses who are living in the year 2015 already and emulate them.

Shed Your Old Winning Strategy.

To create an Impossible Future, you will definitely need to shed your organization's winning strategy. That strategy has allowed your company to be successful in the past, but has become a source of limitation—whether it's selling PCs, coffee, package delivery, or car insurance. It is important to keep in mind that just because one approach has reached its limits, that doesn't mean there isn't an alternative way. Look for people already living in the future and emulate them—in your own terms. Don't sell PCs, sell service (Dell). Don't sell coffee, sell ambiance and a new me in the morning (Starbucks). Don't sell package delivery, sell worldwide logistics and supply chain solutions (UPS). Don't sell insurance, sell speedy claims (Arch Insurance). Don't do operations, do Six Sigma quality (Motorola). But don't be the second or third to sell service instead of PCs or ambiance instead of coffee unless you see a way to do it dramatically better than the first mover; find your own new answer and create your own new market.

Design, Build, Test a Structure for Fulfillment

You create an Impossible Future with passion, courage, and commitment. Yet you also create it by designing a structure for fulfillment that will allow you to actually bring it to pass. Start with the dream, then ask yourself: Where are we now with respect to it?

And—most important—ask yourself: What's missing that will make a difference? This is a whole different question from asking what's needed and wanted—that question leads to limited and specific answers such as time, money, or whatever. Asking what's missing will get you to the factors that will produce what's needed and wanted. For example, what's missing might be an innovative business concept. What's missing might be a new business process not based on paving the old cow paths. What's missing may be wiring your customers into your database. Your structure for fulfillment comes out of putting all the missing pieces together, keeping in mind that you need to optimize the whole, not just the parts.

TEMPLATE FOR ACTION

1. *Ask your team if they feel they are pursuing a future that is inspiring, empowering, and energizing.* At your next team meeting, pull out your organization's goals and ask people if the goals represent an Impossible Future or a predictable future. Also ask if these goals really energize the organization or, yawn, allow it to fall gently to sleep.

2. *Distinguish your organization's winning strategy.* Ask yourself or your group: What is our winning strategy? How is it the source of our organization's success? How does it limit us? What impact does it have on the goals we set, the plans we make, the actions we take? What can we do to break the grip and excel beyond it?

3. *Define an Impossible Future based on exciting new possibilities, not just goals.* Creating an Impossible Future should start with imagining new possibilities for your organization that then become the basis of goal setting. Ask yourself, What would be an Impossible Future in the area of business concept innovation? In the area of production? The supply chain? People and culture?

4. *Set some high goals that raise the bar for your entire organization and stretch people's minds and skills.* Create one to five BHAGs that help move the possibilities you have declared into the realm of reality. I like setting high goals for an organization, not only because it creates a context that pushes people to achieve what is really possible rather than predictable but because the effort required to achieve such goals tends to become the cauldron for human transformation.

5. Bring various people together to create a "strategic architecture"
for achieving the goals. Based on the premise that two heads are
better than one, bring various people together with different perspectives and begin to look at how you will create the Impossible
Future. Pick four or five major components—projects, initiatives—
that you will put into place. This then becomes the strategic
architecture.

diverse managers that get things jump started. What do we do differently?

Chapter 3

Face Reality
Identify What's Missing That, if Provided, Will Produce a Breakthrough

SITUATION: You've declared your strategic intention and made great forward progress. Yet you have hit a wall and need to declare breakdowns to discover what is missing that will produce a breakthrough. *Your masterful coach will offer you a powerful assist.*

Michel in a Coaching Conversation
with a Business Unit Manager

Every morning at six A.M., Martha Hawkins boards a train at Stonington station for the ninety-minute ride into Chicago. Martha, a business unit manager for Quaker, has a standing reservation in the train's "office car," where she can make calls and power up her laptop. The office car enables Martha to hold down a demanding job while being home on time to tend to her busy family.

I was brought in as an executive coach when Martha took over her job as business unit manager. She had a mandate to grow her rice cake snack business, inherited with the acquisition of Chico San, a natural foods manufacturer. The goal was to grow this high-potential snack food business from almost a standing start to a national brand with substantial revenue. Martha had invited me to facilitate the strategic planning session with her group.

People at the session immediately began to plan the launch of their new brand as if it were the next Coca-Cola, with a substantial budget and other assets, assuming that a lot of things were in place that were not really in place. For example, they pictured a top team that was capable of brand management, consumer insights upon which to base a brand advertising campaign, and a product mix that would appeal to the masses, not just consumers of the sort of crunchy granola sold in natural food stores.

I called a time-out and introduced the group to the steps in the Masterful Coaching Strategic Planning Process:

1. Set a stretch goal—say, "a national brand with substantial sales."
2. Do a "What's So" analysis—where are we now in relation to the goal?
3. Figure out what's missing and what's next.

I explained that, after setting a big goal, you need to face reality and know what your starting point is so that you don't make a plan based on mistaken assumptions.

As the stretch goal was already set, we focused on doing the "What's So" to get a handle on where we were at the time, inquiring into what was working and not working and especially into what was missing that, if provided, would produce a breakthrough.

This resulted in a strategic plan that, in addition to the basics, focused on getting the right people—people who could manage the brand—in the right jobs, gaining consumer insights to make effective advertising and tweak the product mix, improving the supply chain's capacity, and getting out in front of grocery chain buyers and making a pitch for shelf space.

Martha and her team successfully launched the brand in the West and went through a rapid growth curve for the first year, while delivering healthy profits. However, when they tried to apply the same strategies and tactics in the Midwest that had worked so well in the Western market, the brand's fortunes started to plummet while eating up a lot of operating capital.

Almost overnight Martha's reputation began to go from hero to goat. "Michel," she said, "it has always been my belief that we have a great strategy and if we stay the course, we will get the results we want. Yet our Midwest numbers show we are missing the boat, what do we do? How do we turn this around?"

I said, "Let's acknowledge the success you have achieved so far. At the same time, when you are sticking to a strategy and pressing hard at doing the same things better and not getting different results, there is always the possibility you are in denial about something, and it is time to wake up, face reality one more time, and gain new insights so that we can do something different. I think doing another 'What's So' focused on the Midwest business is just what the doctor ordered."

 TEACHABLE POINT OF VIEW: To create the future, declare your strategic intent, and then face reality.

You cannot get to the future without a profound acknowledgment and understanding of where you are today.

It is one thing to conjure up a vision of the future that represents what will be, the "global leader in . . . " you name it. But realizing that vision often requires learning a lesson in corporate humility by looking in the mirror and honestly acknowledging where you are today. This involves having the courage to tell the truth about how far you are from reaching the goals and all the missing capabilities that need to be built before you can close the gap. It means uncovering at all levels—and in a way that is visible to everyone concerned—what is actually so about the current reality.

Too often leaders and teams of leaders operate with an inaccurate and incomplete understanding of their current reality. They are out of touch with how things really are in their business and live in a world of assumptions—a world of smoke and mirrors. The consequences are huge. Their decisions and actions are ineffective because they don't address the real issues, and worse, are detrimental because they mobilize capital, people, and resources in the wrong direction.

Let's say your strategic intention is to become number one in your industry. The next step is to gain a shared understanding of current reality by looking at what's been accomplished, what's working and not working, and at what's missing that, if provided, will make a critical difference. The findings and insights from the inquiry become the basis for setting major objectives and milestones, designing key projects, and taking high-leverage actions that will put you on the right track and lead to some early successes. It is equally important to constantly hone the strategy in light of the changing landscape, looking at what progress has been made, what the new learnings are, and what new opportunities are opening up.

Declare a time-out, regroup, and examine where you are and what is missing. Then move into action with powerful new insights and greater energy.

Sometimes people can be reluctant to engage in a process to understand reality, preferring instead to jump into action as quickly as possible. They may regard it as a waste of time or fear that it may be disempowering to those involved. We have found that, in fact, the opposite is true. Sure, facing with sober realism what it will take to reach your goal can bring some initial and temporary dismay, but it is also and ultimately liberating. When you get rid of the false hope that things will automatically turn out the way you intended, you get rid of the hopelessness that often lies just beneath it. It is then that you can begin to identify those crucial missing pieces. Suddenly, the impossible becomes achievable.

When President Kennedy declared that we would put a man on the moon by the end of the decade, the reality of what was missing was overwhelming. From that strategic intent, the NASA scientists had to become totally grounded in current reality. Specifically, they needed to have a clear understanding of all the technological issues that needed to be resolved in order to break away from earth's gravity and to safely return home. They could dream about going to the moon all day long, but without this understanding, they had not a hope of escaping earth's boundaries.

In addition to the invaluable advantage you give yourself and your team by accurately knowing the current terrain, the process of determining together what is actually so serves to powerfully bond the individuals involved, creating connection, alignment, and a deeper relationship among them all. The "What's So" process forces people in the group to have real conversations about the goal, to bring the tough issues to the table, to let go of long-held views and individual interpretations that are the source of separation and also to build a shared understanding that becomes the basis of a shared strategy and effective action.

TEMPLATE FOR ACTION
1. *Plan the "What's So":*
Designate who should attend: Get the right people to participate—those accountable for creating the new future.

Create the categories you will investigate: Slice the business into four or five different categories or "windows for inquiry," to organize the examination. One window should be the business or project as a whole. Other windows could be things such as Marketing, Sales, Strategy, Leadership, Personnel, Culture, Operations, Processes and Systems, and so on. If it is a project, it could be the various work streams. Pick the categories in such a way that everything is captured. The objective is to look into every corner of the business (or project).

Schedule the session: Dedicate the right amount of time. We have found that it usually takes two to four hours for a specific issue or part of the business, and a full day to a day and a half for a business area or an organization.

Establish a time frame for the inquiry: Choose to review the business or project over a specific period of the past—anywhere between three months and three years.

Find a productive setting: Set up the right circumstances for a productive and intense process. For example, no interruptions, off-site if possible.

2. *Prepare people for the "What's So" process:* Explain the process and provide a context for everyone's participation. Talk to people about where you are coming from and where you would like them to come from: "We are here to make a difference. We are here to get to the heart of the matter. We are committed to using this conversation to create a new future." Create a safe environment so that people are willing to open up, tell the truth, and face the difficult issues. There should be no feeling that people's jobs are on the line.

3. *Conduct the "What's So" process:* List the following five questions on a separate flip chart. You will be discussing all of them for each category of the inquiry. As you look at each question, capture the answers on flip charts and tape them on the walls. By the end of the session, you should be surrounded by the "What's So" discoveries.

What are the facts? Facts are indisputable truth—black-and-white information. What are the few relevant and revealing facts that ground everybody and provide insights?

What are the accomplishments so far? Capture anything that anybody considers an accomplishment. It can be quantitative or qualitative, business or people oriented. When you do a great job capturing and acknowledging all accomplishments, it creates a sense of progress and it makes people more willing to engage with the tough questions.

What is working? Or has worked? These are the things that you have observed as key elements, behaviors, or practices that resulted in the accomplishments you just listed—the things that have made a difference so far and have been the triggers for the accomplishments. You want to identify these so that as you go forward and make changes, you can avoid throwing out the baby with the bathwater and ensure that you continue to do those things that are working.

What is not working? Or has not worked? Be as straight and explicit as possible. Bring the conversation deep enough that it results in some powerful insights. Peel the onion by asking questions to make people go beyond their level of thinking so far. Saying, "customer service is not working" is a good start, but not that useful. Go deeper: "What is not working about customer service?" The answer might be: "The way our store staff deals with customers." Dig deeper by asking: "I see, what does not work about how our staff interacts with customers?"

What's missing that, if provided, will produce a breakthrough? This is the most important question in the "What's So" process. The answer is often hidden behind the obvious. "What's missing" in regard to the issue of store staff and poor service, for example, could be hiring more enthusiastic people, providing better customer service training, or making sure every store has a champion for great service.

What are the opportunities presented by the "What's So"? Identifying what is missing leads you directly to some powerful opportunities going forward. Capture all opportunities from the entire inquiry, especially focusing on the "what's missing" question, as it will lead you to the most powerful ones. Opportunities also come from building on what is now working.

4. *Design goals, plans, and high-leverage actions around what's missing.* Look at everything you have designated as opportunities going forward. Turn the opportunities into action. What are the three to five things you want to focus on? What are people eager to get to work on? What will make the most difference? The idea is to break what's missing into small, decisive projects. Look at where you can make something happen so as to create an early success, which will lead to new openings for action and accomplishment.

Chapter 4

Create a Source Document

Vision, Major Milestones, Key Initiatives, Guiding Principles, and Methodologies

SITUATION: It was a terrific vision statement you came up with at the big meeting, but today it is just another good idea gone up in smoke. You keep asking yourself what's missing that will have an impact. *Your masterful coach has a great leadership tool to offer you.*

Robert in a Coaching Conversation with a European Oil Company Leader

The year was 2003. The day Monday, May 5. The time seven o'clock in the morning. The place Boston. The phone rang: "Hello, this is Greg Goff." He was calling in from London for our regularly scheduled coaching call. The news that morning was big, following the merger announcement of Conoco and Phillips. "I have just been given a great promotion."

"Fabulous!" I shouted, thinking this was a stepping-stone toward Greg's chief executive potential. Greg's secretary, Dee Boom, once referred to Greg as a the Greek god. He had enormous leadership potential. He combined vision and a drive to accomplish things that could be electrifying, along with rock-solid character and judgment. His news indicated that he had just achieved the rank of president of ConocoPhillips International Downstream, a business group larger than many Fortune 500 firms.

When I first started working with Greg, my mission was to get him to show up as a leader who could create an extraordinary new future for his entire organization rather than just running the business as most leaders in his industry did. He also needed to transform himself: from a leader who revealed only intellectual brilliance and drive to an emotional leader who could win people's hearts and minds.

I started talking to Greg about what it meant to be the kind of leader who is the source of an organization's future rather than just a steward who polishes up grandma's china and preserves the past. The dictionary defines a *source* as "one who originates something new, or initiates change." Strongly sourced organizations radiate the assurance of inspiring vision and values, game-changing business concepts, and powerful and unique management cultures. He asked for some examples.

I started rattling off, "Steve Jobs is the source of Apple, Bill Gates is the source of Microsoft, Andrew Grove is the source of Intel, Scott McNealy is the source of Sun Microsystems, Jack Welch is the source of today's GE, Sam Walton is the source of Wal-Mart, Richard Branson is the source of Virgin Group, Anita Roddick is the source of The Body Shop, Estee Lauder is source of Estee Lauder Cosmetics, Ned Johnson is the source of Fidelity Investments, and Giorgio Armani is the source of Armani."

Greg said he had the aspiration to be the kind of leader I was talking about, and asked me about the path forward. "How do I transform myself into an extraordinary leader like this?" I said for such a transformation to occur, we needed a kind of alchemical crucible. I said the crucible would be made up of three key components: the creation of a Source Document—a blueprint for the future; executing on what was in the Source Document while still running the day-to-day business, and personal reinvention" from ongoing 360-degree feedback as a prelude to organizational reinvention.

"What do you see as the difference between a Source Document and a typical vision statement?" asked Greg. I suggested that, for one thing, a Source Document has to have someone standing behind it, someone with a powerful intention to initiate change. Greg then pondered a moment and discovered his own answer. "So many vision statements are 'pie in the sky' with no idea of how to bring it down to earth. For me, a Source Document needs to include both the whats and the hows."

"Exactly!" I responded.

TEACHABLE POINT OF VIEW: Create an inspiring Source Document that gets people to stand in the future and guides them to act in the present to make it a reality.

The leaders of strongly sourced organizations come up with innovative business concepts and a powerful and unique enterprise culture—and have a track record of brilliant results.

A Source Document is the leader's declaration of intention to call forth an extraordinary future. It is a manifesto in the form of a written artifact that gives everyone in the organization a shared place to stand: not just an inspiring vision and empowering values, but also a reliable map for achieving that vision. It is the Source Document that allows leaders to mobilize people to take a stand for an extraordinary future. Yet it also enables them to realize it by providing the necessary strategies and major milestones, guiding principles, and key initiatives, methodologies, and actions. Greg's story is a great example.

Greg and I sat down to work on the Source Document in my study, which recreates the formally informal atmosphere of an old-fashioned gentlemen's club, with leather sofas and silver tea service. After a while, the walls were covered with flip charts emblazoned with handwritten scrawls and images that reminded me of Leonardo da Vinci's futuristic yet arcane drawings of the airplane, machine gun, and submarine.

Our original draft of the Source Document showed an inspiring *what*—the "Billion Dollar Challenge"—based on a the idea of creating an inspired, high-performing organization where each person makes a difference. The Source Document also articulated an empowering *how,* starting with some teachable points of view designed to shift culture and guide thinking and behavior in reaching the goals. These rested over something we called the "Golden Pyramid," pictured in Figure 4.1.

Near the end of our first year together, Greg sat in my study, where the original conversational artifacts of the Source Document were back on the wall, and on a conference call to someone in his

**Figure 4.1. The Billion-Dollar Challenge—
A Source Document.**

**Extraordinary
Leaders at All Levels**
*Leaders set significant
business and leadership goals,
and receive coaching and mentoring*

Going for Growth
Through acquisition and organically

Creating a Strong Foundation
*Yearly coaching
reviews*   *Digital dashboard on
key business drivers*   *Six Sigma
quality*

organization to explained what he was up to. He spoke in a matter-of-fact tone, yet in such an inspiring, empowering way that he left little doubt that he had entered the leadership crucible and been transformed by it.

His words came from the inside out, from the soul and the marketplace, not from the outside in, from something he had been told or read. Here was a full-fledged, difference-making leader up to the task of reaching high goals and bringing about transformational change while at the same time expertly managing the transactions of major deals and daily business affairs.

The Source Document inspires people by addressing their needs and timeless values. It also empowers them by providing specific milestones, guiding principles, and methodologies. Here are some of the key elements:

Aspects of a Source Document

- *A statement that engages people:* We are all partners in creating a new future.
- *Unwanted condition:* Lackluster financial performance, dissatisfied customers, employees in a state of profound resignation.
- *Vision:* To create an inspired, high-performing organization that liberates and empowers hundreds of people in the pursuit of an Impossible Future.
- *Empowering values:* For customers: from a *me* point of view to a *you* point of view. For employees: stand for people's success. For shareholders: stewardship.
- *Strategic intent:* To move from niche player to the biggest or the best; to be the most competitive enterprise on earth.
- *Goals:* The entire organization has committed itself to the goal of 10 percent growth per year, 20 percent return on capital employed.
- *Major milestone:* To achieve $350 million in new sales; reduce costs by $350 million through sustainable process improvement.
- *Key initiatives:* To create the next generation of leaders; to develop business concept incubator; to introduce a Six Sigma quality program.
- *Teachable point of view:* You and I can make a difference in meeting the rising aspirations and urgent needs of customers, employees, shareholders.

- *Methodology:* Strategic planning in action—first face reality; next set high goals; and third, provide what's missing that will make a difference.

I want to say something about results. In December 2003, one year after Greg completed his Source Document, he was widely being acknowledged by people throughout his organization as a visionary leader who could execute like mad while maintaining a reputation for fairness in dealing with others. Literally thousands of employees in twenty-three countries joined with him in his quest to create an inspired, high-performing organization by setting up and delivering on significant leadership and business challenges. Finally, the proof is in the numbers. The company achieved a record profit of $325 million and $50 million in sustainable improvements, roughly double that of his predecessor in the previous year, and a record not matched by anyone since the company had started in 1960.

TEMPLATE FOR ACTION

1. *Write a Source Document in a way that engages people.* For example, the Constitution of the United States, which constitutes a magnificent Source Document, does this brilliantly by beginning with the democratic yet magisterial words, "We the people . . ."

2. *Include in the Source Document:*

Your vision and values. Address the stagnating conditions that are producing pent-up frustration for customers, employees, and stakeholders. The Hunger Project Web site says, "In a world awash with food, 20,000 people a day die of hunger."

A strategic intent. Describe the final milestone by which goals are set, planning is done, and action is taken: creating a democratic government, generating a billion dollars in new market value, ending chronic hunger and starvation.

The key change initiatives that are the strategic architecture of organization. These become the basis for hundreds and thousands of ways of participating in making the vision a reality.

Teachable points of view or guiding principles for transforming behavior. This should include specific methodologies for making the entire process successful.

3. *When the Source Document is ready, arrange a number of town hall meetings to get the message through to your organization.* Be determined to put out the message in the Source Document with every breath you take until it becomes the vision, climate, and spirit of the company.

4. *Create the Source Document as a visual artifact to help get the message across and sustain it.* Our client Marks & Spencer worried that if they put their Source Document on a flat paper it would get lost on the desk or if they put it on a PowerPoint it would disappear into the computer. So they developed something called "The Cube," where the vision, mission, values, goals, teachable points of view, and key initiatives were simply and clearly diagramed.

5. *Give everyone a copy of the Source Document.* As conversations disappear from memory, access to the Source Document allows people to inspire and energize themselves again—which will be important when they discover that it is not all smooth sailing on their journey to the future.

6. *Tenaciously follow through.* Make sure you personally embody the ideas, values, and teachable points of view in the Source Document. Make sure you tenaciously follow through on getting the message through to the organization, in taking action toward intended goals, and in powerfully launching key change initiatives.

Exhibit 4.1 lists a number of examples of the elements of a Source Document and of different types of Source Documents.

Exhibit 4.1. Source Document Examples.

Political

The creation of the Declaration of Independence was one of the most powerful acts of transformational leadership in the history of the world. It was created by a galaxy of leaders, including Jefferson, Madison, and Franklin. It started off by proclaiming a list of grievances against the king (and all tyrants) and then envisioned a new nation in which leaders governed by the consent of the governed, guaranteeing the right to life, liberty, and the pursuit of happiness.

The Declaration, with its bold signature by John Hancock and the names of more than two score revolutionary leaders, was publicly proclaimed in Philadelphia on the 4th of July, 1776, read to George Washington and his troops the next day, and dispatched posthaste to the most distant towns and hamlets in the thirteen colonies.

The Declaration set the stage for another "Source Document," the Constitution, and our most precious possession, the Bill of Rights. The Constitution was full of game-changing ideas: it chartered a nation that was based on the peaceful, voluntary transition of vast powers from one group of leaders to another; it embraced the paradox of federal and state government; it created a system of checks and balances.

Business

In 1943, General Robert Wood Johnson, who guided Johnson & Johnson (J&J) from a small, family-owned business to a worldwide enterprise, published the Johnson & Johnson Credo, a one-page document that said J&J was committed to being the leading business in the field of health care products and, to that end, would live by a set of empowering values. To start with: "We believe our first responsibility is to the doctors, nurses and patients, mothers and fathers and all others who use our products first." The Credo, which put customers first, employees second, and stockholders last, received wide public attention and acclaim. J&J employees were able to draw strength from the Credo during the Tylenol crisis (when a few bottles were found tainted with poison), pulling all Tylenol off the shelves in every store, in every country, and restoring J&J's reputation.[1]

Nongovernment Organization

The Hunger Project is a strategic organization and global movement dedicated to unleashing the human spirit for the end of hunger. The

Exhibit 4.1. Source Document Examples, Cont'd.

Hunger Project has a two-pronged strategy: 1) to identify the conditions that give rise to the persistence of hunger and to create strategies to make known and directly intervene and transform these conditions, and 2) to mobilize the self-reliant action of local leadership to clear away obstacles to enable grassroots action to succeed. The core team of the Hunger Project, under the direction of Joan Holmes, has articulated a vision statement for the organization. The vision states their belief that achieving the sustainable end of hunger means nothing less than creating a new future for all humanity, a future where:

- Every day, every person has enough of the right food to be healthy and productive;

- Babies are born healthy and strong, and girl babies are prized as much as boy babies;

- Children stay alive, so parents can have smaller families;

- Women and girls are full partners in society;

- People have control over their own lives and destinies, and all individuals have a chance to contribute;

- The values of honoring human beings and nature flourish.

They have also rigorously articulated a set of principles that, along with the vision, posit an extraordinary future for humanity and are the basis for setting specific goals and key initiatives every year in partnership with people in a dozen far-flung countries.[2]

Chapter 5

Get Everyone to Formulate a Significant Business Challenge

Create Line of Sight to Strategic Goals

SITUATION: You want to create focus and energy around your strategic goals and priorities. People say they want to focus on things that make a difference, but they are bogged down in a laundry list of objectives. *Here's a proven method that will pay off in spades.*

Michel in a Coaching Conversation with an Electronics Executive

I am sitting in a small conference room in Zurich, gazing idly at the giant head of a Swiss elk mounted on the wall and sipping dark coffee, waiting for a meeting with Lothar Hansen, chief executive of a tier-two electronic components manufacturer and an expert at hunting down business deals. As Lothar breezes in, he salutes me and announces that we only have twenty minutes. "Michel, what can I do for you?" Lothar has piercing eyes, speaks with a lot of edge, and always seems to be impatient to do the next thing on his agenda.

I waste no time. "I am meeting with your entire leadership team in the next three days to work on formulating their business challenge in a series of individual coaching sessions. I would like to gain your perspective on how I can make the biggest impact in my sessions with your people." Lothar reflects for less than thirty seconds: "Here is the deal. What I want in my organization is to dramatically increase the number of people in leadership positions who are truly and actively making a difference."

"What exactly do you mean by 'making a difference'? What would that look like?"

"Simple. It means two things. First, it means everyone doing a great job of running the business. Every person has ten to twenty goals and objectives for the year and it means reaching those goals. These guys are all capable and experienced and, the truth is, I have total confidence that they will get the job done on that front. Second, I want everyone to take on and produce some kind of breakthrough in the business. As you call it, a 'significant business challenge.' I mean that people pick a high-leverage area in their business and they create a step change."

Lothar sits up in the leather chair and looks me straight in the eyes. "This is where my leaders are weak. Most are not currently working on making something new happen, nor do they know how to do that. It would be worth gold to me if I had fifty to one hundred leaders highly capable and focused on delivering significant new business breakthroughs. Michel, that is where my team needs your support."

"Ten four!"

◆　◆　◆

The next day, my first coaching session is with Jeffrey Horowitz, Lothar's marketing director, and it takes no time to confirm Lothar's insights. When I offer to help Jeffrey identify and develop his significant business challenge, he quickly embraces the suggestion. "Great idea! Lothar wants us all to make a presentation of our significant business challenge at the next leadership team meeting in three weeks and I welcome the help. I am not clear how to go about this."

I start, "Jeffrey, let's first define what a significant business challenge is. From my experience there are four factors that distinguish a significant business challenge from a normal goal. One, it is something that will make a new and significant contribution to the business. Two, it is something that is unprecedented and unpredictable. Three, it is something that will challenge you and others to step up and think and act differently. And four, it is something that you can take on with passion.

"All your goals are important, but the one you choose for this needs to stand out. If at any point, this challenge becomes just one of the other goals on your list, you will fail. To deliver a breakthrough requires a different level of focus, attention, and intention. It takes leadership." I paused, letting it sink in. "When I give you these criteria, what comes to your mind?"

Jeffrey's eyes sparkle. "There is an area in my business where I see I can make a unique difference. And I could actually be very passionate about this."

"Great, tell me more and we will begin to formulate your significant business challenge. I want us to do a superb job formulating this challenge. To get it right, we need to use an iterative approach. The clearer you can identify, powerfully articulate, and then communicate your challenge, the more likely you will be successful a year from now. Let's go to work."

TEACHABLE POINT OF VIEW: Create line of sight to the "Grand Design" by asking people to come up with significant business challenges.

*Are you up for a challenge that will stimulate your
imagination, test your mettle, enhance your aliveness?*

You have defined an Impossible Future and big game for yourself to play. Coming up with significant business challenges is an
excellent way to get people to show up as players, as well as to take
a dream that looks like pie in the sky and begin to bring it down
to earth. A significant business challenge can take several different
forms. For example, it can look like a big goal or problem to be
solved. On the other hand, it can also take the form of a fascinating and intriguing project that you can't wait to get to work on in
the morning. In formulating a significant business challenge, it's
important to keep two questions in front of you at all times. Will it
produce a breakthrough in results? Will it produce a breakthrough
for people?

*Think in terms of exciting new possibilities and then set
high goals undimmed by precedent.*

The process of reaching a breakthrough has three main stages:
formulation, concentration, and momentum. We are going to
focus here on the first stage. Formulation accounts for 50 percent
of your eventual success. Most people think that success on any
project or endeavor comes from the realm of action, so they are in
a hurry to get going. But if you formulate well, you bring power
and velocity to reaching the goals and waste less time in futile activities. In the high-pressure environment of today, people are so
action oriented that they almost never want to spend the proper
amount of time in formulating. Typically people want to spend
only a day or a week at most formulating. We recommend that, if
you are going to spend a year on a project, you should spend one
to two months formulating well—then the next ten or so months
will be much more productive.

*Design projects that fascinate, intrigue, and that you
can't bear to put down at night.*

The Masterful Coaching Methodology

To formulate successfully, you need to have a rigorous methodology. Our methodology, which we have applied in hundreds of situations, is simple but effective. It supports you in setting goals where your eyes are undimmed by precedent, and that can only be achieved, not by thinking outside the box but by burning it. It challenges you to get clear on both the what and the how, and provides a means to coaching people in action until their goals are reached.

The formulation process needs to bring clarity to seven distinct questions.

- What difference will your breakthrough make for the business?
- What will success look like? How will you measure it?
- What are the key things you will do to be successful?
- Who are the people who will be critical in various ways to your success?
- What actions will make the most difference in starting out with a bang?
- Is the goal a transformational opportunity for you and your organization?
- Does the journey look like it will be fun?

TEMPLATE FOR ACTION

1. *Align with your boss on a business breakthrough.* Sit down with your boss for sixty to ninety minutes and look at your goals for the year and evaluate them in terms of the following breakthrough criteria: What goal, if any, will make the biggest difference for the organization? What will be the biggest challenge and will truly be a breakthrough? Where is there the most leverage? Make sure that you and your boss are completely in alignment and that you both have a passion for achieving a breakthrough in the area that you have identified.

2. *Use the following methodology to formulate your breakthrough:*

Make a commitment statement: Begin to describe your breakthrough in powerful terms. Use an iterative process—that is, come up with a statement, then question it, and then refine it again. Ask, Is it what is needed and wanted? How will it make or save the company money? Is it big enough or too big? Will it evoke commitment from others? Is it measurable? Will you know when you achieve it? Here are some examples of breakthrough goals: "We will be the premier integrated regional fuels business in Central Europe by the end of 2005." "We will achieve a position of undisputed market leadership. Our competitive differentiation will come from a seamless low-cost value chain and customer focus that is unparalleled in our industry."

Conditions of satisfaction: Clarify how you will define success. Make four to six bullet points that show how the breakthrough goal is measurable. Some points will be more concrete, with numerical targets, and others more subjective, but they should all be clear for you and for everyone else involved. You will find that going through the process of articulating these targets is a process of negotiation. Here are some examples of useful condition of satisfaction statements: "Yields a marketing return on capital employed exceeding 30 percent." "Has a value chain to the end customer with full-cost breakeven of 11 cents per gallon." "Achieves a #1 share in our core markets." "Has all marketing leaders coached to an A level." "Grows from 127 to 245 stores by 2005."

Structure for fulfillment: Identify the main area of focus or main activities that you will have to address. A good question: What is missing in order to be successful? For example, when we wanted to put a man on the moon, what was missing was a material that could handle the heat upon reentry into earth's atmosphere. Of course many other things needed to be done, but this one was critical. You should have no more than four to eight critical items—not a to-do list that attempts to cover everything.

Critical people for success: Every time you produce a breakthrough, a lot of people play a critical role. It is important to identify these people and what kind of relationship you need to create with them. Ask, Who needs to play an implementation role, a support role, or a political role? Who needs to give their blessing? Who might be a barrier or play an opposition role? This then becomes a "relationships map."

Key actions for success: Review your structure for fulfillment and your critical people for success and identify actions that will get you quickly into the game. Focus on doable actions and small wins. Get something accomplished and under your belt that can create a widening circle of success. Avoid letting too much time lapse between formulation and action. Capitalize on the power of clarity that is available in the formulation phase and launch into action immediately.

3. *Schedule a review of breakthrough commitments.* Commit to a monthly review that you will do with yourself or with others. Put it on your calendar. It's like sailing a boat—as conditions change, you must make adjustments to your course. If you do not have a monthly review, you will not succeed. In the review ask yourself the following questions: What has been accomplished? What is working and what is not working? What issues and dilemmas are arising? What is missing? What is next that will make a difference?

Chapter 6

Desperate to Break Out of the No-Growth Morass?

Blow Up Your Business Model
Versus Tinker at the Margins

 SITUATION: You face a dilemma. Either blow up your business model and come up with new wealth-creating strategies or continue tinkering at the margins despite diminishing returns. *We'll guide you in getting to the core of your dilemma and cracking it open.*

Robert in a Coaching Conversation with a Leader of an International Household Products Company

Dan Powers was vice president of a company that competed with Procter & Gamble on household cleaning products like Tide, Ajax, Mr. Clean, and Fantastik. Powers and his company faced a real business problem: achieving top-line growth with multiple brands in a market overcrowded with competition. Just walk into Walgreen's or any supermarket and you will see the shelves packed with dozens of me-too products like the ones he was trying to sell.

Dan explained to me when we started working together that they had in the past year embarked on an ambitious corporate-wide initiative they called "Fast Growth" to address this issue. The program started with a strategic challenge of growing the business by 12 percent. They also created a strategic architecture for achieving this based on four "big rocks": brand compression—(building leading brands and divesting weaker ones), regenerating the core business by selling more to existing customers, coming up with game-changer ideas that would open new opportunities for creating wealth, and designing a leadership development program aimed at producing growth leaders and an entrepreneurial culture. Yet, in spite of all this, growth seemed to elude them.

I told Dan that, on the surface, they seemed to be doing everything brilliantly. I asked him to let me do a quick discovery process or a "What's So" on what was really going on, which would consist of interviewing people at various levels of the organization. The intention would be to come up with some insights about the no-growth morass and possible ways out by distinguishing the problem, the cause, the solution (what was missing), and any next steps.

"My preliminary observation," I told Dan after doing the interviews, "revealed four points. One, your business is still profitable based on tinkering with selling brands off and continuous improvement, but you are not doing anything radically different to create and sustain new wealth. Two, you want a fast-growth culture, but your top managers are in fact forcing people to breathe the stale air of orthodoxy when they come up with world-shaking ideas. Three, you don't seem to have any alignment around what the problem is or the solution that will put you on the path to growth. And four, your people haven't tasted success in a while and, furthermore, have not been paid bonuses as a result of the lack of growth. They are frustrated, infuriated, and resigned."

Dan sighed. "Doctor, is there a way out for us?" he asked.

I said, "Dan, our point of view at Masterful Coaching is that anything is possible, there is always a path forward, and everything is transformable."

He then asked me if I had any other insights that could help with the no-growth morass. "Just one other thing," I said, a little bit like Lieutenant Columbo, Peter Falk's TV detective, "One of the people I talked to in the company said something that got me thinking: 'We all keep believing that if we all do what we have always been excellent at, it will all go into a black magic box and we will grow. We are making an assumption that we are on the right track and I don't think we really are.'"

When he asked me what I suggested, I told him, "I think we need to have a Breakthrough Meeting where we get all the stakeholders in the same room and look for the path to growth. We can start with some provocative questions that must be answered with a commitment to the truth. For example, do you think that our once-successful business model has reached the point of diminishing returns and that we are in denial? Is it time to blow up our business model or can we still get away with tinkering at the margins? What opportunities do we have to engage in business concept innovation based on satisfying new or existing customer needs and wants? What is the best path to growth within our core business, and the simple and logical basic things that we need to get better at doing?"

TEACHABLE POINT OF VIEW: Do something different rather than just doing something better.

> *Leaders of companies with once-successful business*
> *models ought to go on trial for being in denial long after*
> *they have reached the point of diminishing returns.*

Today every company needs to grow, and it is important to take the point of view that every business is a growth business, whether you are a company like Coca-Cola, a seller of fast foods like McDonald's, or a maker of sophisticated computer systems like Sun Microsystems. The issue, according to Gary Hamel, is that in a turbulent world—where incumbency is worth less than ever—you get to a point where your business model collapses under the pressure of new competitors fresh from the niche and you reach a point of diminishing returns.

> *Blow up your business model, don't tinker at the*
> *margins. It is easier to create a Wal-Mart than it is*
> *to change a Sears.*

The issue for many companies is not just coming up with a strategic challenge and new strategic options that will produce growth, it is altering a managerial frame of mind that is rooted in the past and thereby gets caught in denial, arrogance, and nostalgia. For example, Coca-Cola had difficulty getting more "share of throat" by selling brown sugar water. McDonald's is having difficulty building sales to a burger-weary public. Sun Microsystems, once a top growth company, arrogantly pursued its "server strategy" directly in the face of evidence that servers were being commoditized by companies like Dell and that operating software was being blown away by Linux.

Re-Imagine Your Business

> *Focus on getting different instead of getting better.*

Most companies today, says Hamel, can't grow revenue by flogging the same old stuff to the same old customers through the same old channels in the same old way. People may already be drinking as much fizzy water as they are ever going to drink, eating as many hamburgers as they are ever going to eat, drinking as much beer as they are ever going to drink, wearing as much deodorant and antiperspirant as they are ever going to wear. This fact may make you sad, but at the same time it can be liberating. The challenge for many companies is not getting better at what they are already doing, but rather getting different, which means doing something else, which implies innovation.

The only way out of the no-growth morass might be freaky innovation. When most companies think of innovation, they tend to think of product innovation, not coming up with innovative business concepts. For example, Gillette people came up with the safety razor with one blade. In hopes of growing the business, they next came up with the Track Razor with two blades, which did improve revenues as customers threw out their old single blade in favor of the new version. Next they came up with another razor with three blades, which had less impact on revenue, and now they are coming up with a razor with four blades.

Yes, We Hear You

You do need to be two-headed about this—you need both "business innovation" and "regenerating your core business." You cannot expect to grow revenues without coming up with innovative business concepts, jaw-dropping new products, or services that directly address what gets people pissed off with existing companies. For example, Dell did this with made-to-order PCs, then later with shifting from PCs to servers when the PC market became commoditized. DoCoMo, the Japanese cell phone company, did this by taking the traditional cell phone and providing iMode service with news briefs, downloadable songs, and location-based services—like finding out where the nearest pizza place is from where you are standing. Boston has a free paper called the *Metro* that is making big profits and dramatically reducing the sales of the *Boston Globe* and *Boston Herald*. The question is, how do you make sure this kind of innovation happens by design, not accident?

TEMPLATE FOR ACTION

1. *Set a growth aspiration that is inspirational, realizable, and nonnegotiable.* The idea behind this is to put a stake in the ground that says we are serious about achieving profitable growth on a sustainable basis. And then hold the line—refuse to reduce your aspiration in the face of no results. You can predict that people's first line of attack will be to sell the same old thing, more or less the same old way, to the same old channels with some modest embellishments. It is important that, in the event that initial efforts don't work out, your stand for your aspiration is nonnegotiable. This will force people to think creatively to come up with ideas that will generate growth.

2. *Get out of denial, nostalgia, and arrogance by doing a "What's So" analysis.* There is never an absence of available solutions to growing your business when it reaches the point of diminishing returns, but given that the senior management is likely to be in denial, nostalgia, and arrogance, none of the solutions will work. It is therefore vital to not only set the high-growth aspiration but to do a "What's So" process that will get people to face reality. For example, here's a useful line of questioning: You say your growth goal with your present brands is 12 percent. The market in your categories is only growing by 6 percent and your chief competitor (who has had a first mover advantage) is also struggling. Please tell us how you expect to reach your goal of 12 percent, or even 6 percent, by simply getting better at what you are already doing. When people can't come up with the answer to this request, they'll hear you when you point out that they need to not just do better but get different.

3. *Ask outsiders or radical thinkers to review senior management's strategy, plans, and budget and present an alternative view.* One of the major hurdles to overcome in fostering innovative strategies in the service of growth is the fact that senior management often tends to take the orthodox view. This is not surprising—they have been there the longest and are likely to be the authors of that view. To counteract this tendency, it's important to give senior management, especially those who control the purse strings, an alternative view. An easy way to do this is to invite a group of knowledgeable outsiders from the

edges of your industry to review the strategies, or to invite a group of internal high-flyers with a reputation for radical thinking to review it.

4. *Hold a collaborative gathering on "The Path to Growth."* Bring people together from across your organization and invite them to use their different views and perspectives to light creative sparks and brainstorm on the following proposition: How do we achieve profit-able growth on a sustainable basis? For the core business, ask: Where can we find truly novel opportunities for core business growth? What approaches have been tried in the past? Why did these succeed or fail and what was learned? What are the most powerful tools and methods for identifying profitable options going forward? For new business concepts, ask: What are some new wealth-creating opportunities? What are some market spaces where big customer needs are going unsatisfied? What are the shadows cast by the orthodoxies of an industry or business function?

5. *Set up a game-changer process based on a thousand ideas, a hun-dred experiments, and ten new businesses.* In many companies new ideas are often choked off by senior leaders who are the authors of the status quo and thereby its defenders. One way to deal with this is to set up an alternative way to present innovative growth ideas and get them funded. The leaders need to set the stage by making it known that you want to get every growth idea that people have. Every leader in every business unit, category, or brand needs to get the message to encourage people to come up with at least a hundred ideas and ten breakthrough projects. The best ideas are selected and reviewed by a committee of peers. People are given encouragement and enough resources to get going.

Make sure people get the message they are to be working on something radical. Put it in people's goals that they are supposed to be spending no more than 70 percent of their time on core business stuff and at least 30 percent of their time working on experiments or breakthrough projects that are considered radical in service of growth. All leaders or managers need to have coaching sessions with their direct reports to make sure the ideas are radical enough, and yet not so far afield as to be irrelevant.

Fund innovative experiments by putting aside 10 percent of your present budget. It doesn't make a lot of sense to try to run every idea for an experiment up to the executive committee of your company. Instead, ask every manager to create a yearly budget and plan that includes apportioning 5 to 10 percent of capital on experiments that might illuminate the path to growth. Each experiment should cost in the neighborhood of $10,000 to $30,000.

Create a game-changer review with the board to take successful experiments to the next level. For this review, the key managers all ask their groups to present the results of their best growth experiments to the executive group, which selects the ideas to be taken to the next level in terms of new marketing strategies, game-changing products, and innovative business concepts. The winners are funded; the losers are thanked.

Use a team-based coaching approach based on a widening circle of small successes. One way to break out of the no-growth morass is to go for a small success and then create a widening circle of successes. Each success boosts confidence and morale, and it results in learning something that can be a spearhead for a larger breakthrough. Start with a challenging but attainable goal of making or saving the company money in the next 120 days. Transform this into a project that opens up new possibilities and is doable. For example, instead of trying to grow an entire category, say, face cream, think in terms of growing one brand within it, like Oil of Olay. Load the project for success with what we call "zest factors": success is near and clear, the plan is realizable, the existing resources and authority are enough to go on with, the people are enthusiastic about it, and it's supported by team-based action coaching.

Chapter 7

Looking to Get a Chunk of Capital at Your Next Board Meeting?

The Best Presentation Is the One You Never Make

SITUATION: You have a plan to grow your profitable business, but to do that, you need capital from the CEO and executive committee. Recent attempts to convince the CEO to give money to high-flying growth ideas have met with resistance or been shot down. How are you going to approach your upcoming meeting? *Let us help you.*

Robert in a Coaching Conversation with a Sports Company Marketing Leader

It is 11:58 P.M. and I am sitting with my wife in the bar of the Grand Hotel in Munich, drinking a tall stein of Lobkowicz, a rich Pilsner beer. The clock strikes and in strolls Rob Strasse, marketing chief of Adidas, the person I had spent a good part of the day coaching. He says hello with a broad grin, asks to join us for a Pilsner, and then, after I ask him how his day of negotiations went, proclaims humbly, "I am a genius! The meeting was a huge success."

Rob was heading up a project intended to provide some strategic resilience to Adidas with a new brand strategy called Adidas Equipment. The plan called for rebuilding the brand by focusing on its heritage—providing athletes with equipment instead of catering to fashion. This required not just a new advertising campaign but also new lines of sport shoes and textiles, as well as new sourcing and distribution channels. The idea was that by advertising 3 percent of the Adidas product line as Equipment, it would spearhead a breakthrough for the other 97 percent. The issue was cost—the program would cost $100 million.

Rob came to me and asked for some coaching on the presentation he was about to make to the board of the AG company in Herzogenaurach, Germany. He pulled out a hundred-slide Power-Point presentation and started to launch into it. "Hey, Rob, time out," I said to stop him. "Before you go any further, let's talk about how to 'speak to the listening' of your company chairman and other people in the room." I was well aware that the chairman often doesn't have a lot of imagination when it comes to making big investments in newfangled ideas. Further, he has the disconcerting habit of falling asleep in PowerPoint presentations for chunks of time. Then he wakes up and gives either a thumbs-up or thumbs-down with little or no discussion, without anyone knowing what his thinking is.

I told Rob, "Your idea for Adidas Equipment is great," then added somewhat provocatively, "but you'd better be prepared to throw your presentation in the wastebasket." He asked what I meant. I said, "Sometimes the best presentation is the one you never make."

"You've got my attention," Rob said. "Tell me more."

TEACHABLE POINT OF VIEW: Shift from making a PowerPoint presentation to orchestrating a conversation.

Instead of spending a month in your cubicle on your PowerPoint presentation in virtual isolation, spend that month focused on infiltrating the executive committee.

It happens in every company. People who are activists come up with a big deal revolutionary business idea or sweeping change initiative, then spend weeks or months in isolation slaving over a presentation designed to get the CEO to give them the capital budget to fund it. The strategy is to get on the executive committee's agenda with a powerfully positioned argument set in the company's official PowerPoint background, advocating for your proposal with irrefutable logic and undeniable facts. The dream is that by the time you get to slide 27, the CEO will stand up and say, "Gentlemen, we would be fools not to invest in this!"

Great fantasy. The reality is that this only works, maybe at best, one out of five times. One issue is perhaps that having spent so much time in isolation iterating your presentation, you have not spent enough time infiltrating the board to campaign for your idea. Another issue is that you will tend to talk too much, spending too much time advocating for your ideas and not enough time inquiring into people's concerns and then addressing them. Finally, you need to realize is that it is too risky to be too quick in getting in front of the board with your carefully prepared slides for an all-or-nothing yes/no decision.

Balance Passionate Advocacy with Inquiry

It pays to listen more than you talk. That's why we say, "The most convincing presentation is the one you never make." That is, rather than thinking in terms of making a presentation, start thinking in terms of having a conversation or network of conversations. Instead of spending all your time preparing in isolation, come out and infiltrate—

talk with people on the executive team who can yank the levers of power. Keep in mind that your capital request is eventually going to have to come out of someone's hide, and you need those people to be allies.

When it comes down to the big meeting with the CEO and the executive group, our advice is to send a two- to three-page executive summary in advance that states the opportunity in your proposal, together with any relevant facts, then presents proof that your proposal is executable, reasons why it is urgent to do this now, and how much it will cost. Tell the CEO's executive assistant that you will be sending this so you can spend more time on a real conversation at the upcoming meeting. If you want, have a ten-slide presentation on hand as backup.

In campaigning for your idea and budget request, don't try to change the way people think; do something that awes them so that you change the way they feel. Think about the impending conversation as 20 percent campaigning for your idea with seductive arguments and 80 percent negotiating. For example, Louis Grossman of IBM had the idea for IBM "e-business." Gerstner, the chief executive, had almost outlawed PowerPoint presentations at Big Blue, so Grossman didn't have one on hand when it came time for the big meeting. Instead, Grossman managed to engineer an Internet demo for Gerstner. Moments later, when Gerstner's likeness spoke from a Web page to a throng of IBM senior managers, the e-business die was cast and Grossman got his capital budget.[1]

Make the Negotiation an Enjoyable Exercise in Creative Problem Solving

As far as the negotiation part is concerned, let's take the best-case scenario and assume that the chief executive and others love your proposal. Nonetheless, given scarce resources (and resources are always scarce), they will be weighing the benefits of your proposal against others you will be competing against. The question in their minds at this point is not whether or not they want to do it, but rather how much is it going to cost. So you will be in a negotiation, whether you realize it or not. Negotiation is the art of compromise. You will probably not get everything you want, and you need to be prepared to reframe your proposal accordingly, so as to get the most bang for the buck.

In a presentation you try to subtly convince and persuade. In a conversation you listen to find out what others think. This is key to successful negotiation. You need to hang in the conversation long enough with people with different positions, until all the underlying interests begin to coalesce. For example, the story goes that Bob Kraft, owner of the New England Patriots football team, said to his star quarterback Drew Bledsoe, "We have 30 million to spend in signing players. I am willing to pay you big bucks, because you could make this franchise. So you tell me the amount of money it is going to take me to sign you, and still have enough left over to build a team around you."[2]

TEMPLATE FOR ACTION

1. *Don't isolate; infiltrate.* A good month or so before the big meeting, ask executive assistants, chief adjutants, and bag rats to set some time aside on the executive's calendar to sound them out on a really big opportunity (your idea). Think about the executive's goals, aspirations, and concerns so you will be able to speak in their own terms. Your goal is to find powerful people who have enough at stake in your project to become allies.

2. *Send a short briefing document in advance of the big board meeting.* The briefing document should say why your idea is a great idea, not just a good idea, and why your capital request makes sense in dollars and cents. As you create the briefing document, imagine you are in an actual conversation, anticipating the questions people will ask and answering them just as they come into their mind.

3. *Build social capital with small talk in order to get financial capital with harder talk.* Some great questions to ask: "How's life?" "How's the family?" or "What's on your mind?" As you engage people in this kind of conversation, you will automatically begin building the shared human understandings necessary to bond with them. If you begin the conversation with something like, "Let's cut to the chase," or "Let's just get to the bottom line," people will get the feeling that you are a mercenary. After a few minutes of small talk, ask, "Did you have a chance to look at the briefing document? What did you think?"

4. *Instead of changing how people think about your idea with mind-numbing slides, change how people feel with a demonstration.* We

heard of a purchasing leader of a pharmaceuticals company who wanted to create an "integrated sourcing" program that entailed getting economies of scale by reducing suppliers. The purchasing manager knew the program was enticing, but it needed funding. How could he get the board excited about purchasing? Then he had a Eureka moment! He asked his team to go around the company and collect all the different brands of rubber gloves being used. On the day of the big board meeting, he didn't present one PowerPoint slide. Instead he spoke for about a minute and then put forty-nine pairs of rubber gloves on the boardroom table, each with a different supplier and price label on it. His capital request was granted minutes later.

5. *Listen more than talk; take notes even if what others are saying is gibberish.* It is a good idea to say just a few things about your great idea, and then spend more time listening than talking. "I've said enough. What do you think?" We suggest talking notes on everything others say, even if it sounds like gibberish. This will give people the feeling that what they are saying is important and, at the same time, ensure that you are really listening. This allows you to get vital clues as to people's thinking and to reframe what you are saying so that it speaks to their listening.

6. *Never argue—solve the problem.* Start by showing that you have listened. "From my narrow perspective, I can understand your position that not all business growth is good. But, as the prophet Isaiah once said, 'Come, let us reason together.' Could we creatively solve the problem of 'profitable growth,' perhaps by opening stores in new cities (or countries) that have attractive properties, at good prices and tax advantages? Perhaps you will have some other ways to build on these ideas."

7. *Get a thumbs-up on your capital budget by paying attention to these three factors:*

Time invested. View the capital budgeting process as a series of iterative conversations, rather than an all-or-nothing deal. The more time executives spend reviewing your project, the more likely they are to invest in it to get some payback.

Basis of comparison. We have shopped three suppliers for the new technology and this is by far the best price.

A deadline. Our option on this deal runs out by nine tomorrow morning.

8. *Make concessions grudgingly, asking for something in return.* It's a good idea to start with a bottom-line asking price for delivering on your project. Keep in mind in negotiating that concessions granted too easily are not appreciated. So make concessions grudgingly. If you have to reduce your capital request, do so in larger increments, then smaller ones. "Okay, we can do it for $20 million," later $18 million, later $16.5 million or $15.8 million. This will tell people you have reached the bottom line beyond which the project doesn't make sense. "Now that we are pulling in our belts on this, can I ask your permission to come back and talk to you about this budget again in three months after we have some results to show for it?"

Chapter 8

Create Customers Who Brag About You

Shift from a "Me" Point of View to a "You" Point of View

SITUATION: The people in your company have fallen in love with your advertising, products, and rules. However, they forgot to fall in love with your customers, ignoring their rising needs and expectations. *Here is a golden nugget to transform this situation.*

Robert in a Coaching Conversation with an Airline Marketing Vice President

Freida Radford and I strolled through the decadent Neiderdorf section of Zurich—surrounded by medieval churches, swank hotels, pizza joints, and strip bars. Freida is vice president of the SWISS (previously the bankrupt SwissAir) marketing group. She said, "The issue is that most people who run businesses are not aware that their number one objective is to create and retain customers. You run a great ad campaign and send special promotions out in the mail, but I believe that to lock customers in and lock competitors out, you have to create a customer-centered organization."

I told Frieda, "I have discovered that most companies operate from a 'me' point of view with respect to their customers—that is, based on their policies and procedures—instead of from a 'you' point of view based on the customers' rising needs and expectations." Just then we stopped in an ice cream shop where I asked for a chocolate and vanilla cone. The smiling Swiss matron told me, "We don't do that. You can have chocolate or you can have vanilla. We don't do chocolate and vanilla." When I asked why, she replied, "We have our rules."

Frieda smiled wryly and said, "I guess that's a good example of what you were talking about, but do you think this concept could make a difference at an airline?"

"Of course," I responded, "Can you name me one airline that people actually go out of their way to travel on, on a regular basis?"

"No!"

"Can you name me an airline that you have made a sacred oath with yourself and others never to use again?"

"Yes, at least a half dozen, I'm sure."

She pointed out that at SWISS, many employees have a big smile and a friendly attitude and think they provide great customer service, at least according to the books. However, they tend to puff up like toads when customers make special requests because they are terribly rule-bound. Things like changing your ticket to a flight an hour later, finding the right adaptor to power up your laptop, or asking for something as simple as a magazine if you are flying in economy can put people into a real tizzy.

"Robert, the problem is not that they do or don't give great customer service. The problem is that they actually believe they do. Yet it is as you say, from a 'me' point of view, coming from their perspective and their rules, not from a 'you' point of view. Is it possible to shift this mindset," she asked, "so that people listen to the voice of the customer?"

I responded that it's not only possible to shift this mindset so that it impacts customer service, but also so that it impacts such things as your customer interface, product quality, distribution channels, and more. Frieda responded, "Tell me more."

TEACHABLE POINT OF VIEW: To create customers, shift from a "me" point of view to a "you" point of view.

One of the main opportunities for a preemptive strike on your competition is pissed-off customers. To realize goals like "profitable growth," a leader needs to put out a teachable point of view (or distinction) that fundamentally shifts people's thinking and consequently their behavior. And one of the distinctions that will do most to shift employee attitudes so their behavior is consistent with the goal of creating and sustaining customers is to get everyone in your organization to understand the difference between a "me" point of view and a "you" point of view. This becomes the basis of providing customers with great customer experiences.

The relentless pursuit of a great customer experience can open the way for the radical rebirth of your company's strategy. What's needed is to work from the customer's point of view in, rather than from the point of view of your products and processes out.

I often liken making the shift from a "me" point of view to a "you" point of view to the experience of falling in love—an experience in which studied selfishness transforms into generosity of spirit. All of a sudden you go from being a self-centered clod expecting the world to devote itself to making you happy to being centered around the other person's happiness and going to almost absurd lengths to please, satisfy, and fulfill every heart's desire.

Many business leaders fall in love, but with the wrong thing. They fall in love with their company. They fall in love with their products and service. They fall in love with their customer service policy and all the rules they expect customers to follow. What they need to do is to fall in love with their customers, which naturally leads to the desire to care for them. One way to encourage this kind of relationship is to have the leadership of your organization commit to providing customers with an amazing customer experience. This can lead to a rebirth in your company's strategy and perhaps begin to change the game for your whole industry. Here are some examples:

Virgin Atlantic

Richard Branson, chairman of Virgin Atlantic, says his company is successful not just because it offers "grazing food" in business class throughout the flight, chair massages and manicures, limo service, and so on, but also, "Because I can separate myself from our products and services and empathize with my customers, based on having a clear sense of how I would like to be treated if I was in their shoes."[1] Branson constantly preaches to employees that their business is about creating unforgettable moments for customers. Once you've got that sort of outlook established, watch for people to act accordingly. When someone does something that surprises and delights customers, spread the word and adopt it as a best practice.

Commerce Bank

Sunday morning in the town of Gloucester, New Jersey, is like Sunday morning in any other town—except in the lobby of Commerce Bank, where a dozen or so customers are huddled. The bank is not open "banker's hours" (9 A.M. to 4 P.M.), but "customer's hours" (7:30 A.M. to 8 P.M.) on most days and on weekends as well. A woman is there to deposit money into her sister's bank account so she can get health insurance. An unshaven man in sweats is there with his kids to empty sandwich bags full of change into the change counting machine. "This," says one elderly customer, "is the way banking should be."

Black and Decker

One of my favorite stories about this company (which stands for great products and services) is about the process of designing a new electric grinder to be used in small factory machine shops. The marketing department wanted a distinctive brand look to the design. The engineering department disagreed and believed that the customers wanted a more powerful motor in the drill, more revolutions per minute. Unable to reach an agreement, the sales organization took the drill to a customer site to make sure the drill design wasn't based on a "me" point of view, but a "you" point of view.

As it turned out, the customers didn't care much about the brand label, and they didn't care much about the powerful motor with the faster RPMs. What they wanted was a new protective guard on the drill that would prevent their hands from coming into contact with the grinding wheel. The company then made providing this the highest priority.

 TEMPLATE FOR ACTION

1. *Sound the tone.* Clearly and powerfully communicate to everyone in your organization that your number one objective is to create and sustain customers. Then talk to them about the fact that this will require a shift in who people are being, which will come from taking a stand for customers and drawing their identity from that stand. It also requires a shift in how they are thinking, from a "me" point of view to a "you" point of view. This will not only serve to create a customer-centric organization, it will also lead to such things as innovative product design, quality service, and more effective use of multiple distribution channels.

2. *Learn from other companies that do it well—and from those that don't.* Hold a collaborative session with people from all departments in your firm on creating and sustaining customers. Ask people to come up with a list of ten examples of companies that operate from a self-centered point of view. Then create a list of companies that operate from a customer point of view. Then see what you can learn from these examples as it applies to your company's products and services.

3. *Turn customer frustration with poor service into a competitive weapon.* Do a rigorous inquiry. What happens at the customer interface with your business that really bothers people? What are the customer service policies or rules that drive customers up the wall?

Think about experiences such as standing in line at an airport, being told by your car insurance company that they have a rule that you can't collect your claim on an accident unless you file a police report, or comforting your grandmother when she complains that her new e-mail service is full of spam messages on how to enlarge her penis.

4. Exploit customer dissatisfaction with your industry's products. Ask yourself, What are the chief dissatisfiers and sources of frustration customers have with our industry's products or approach? Then ask yourself, What's missing that, if provided, would make a difference? A group at Procter & Gamble making this inquiry discovered piles of clothes in the backs of people's cars and closets, which told them customers hated going to the dry cleaner. They then invented a game-changing idea that consisted of a home dry cleaning product called Dryel, which has the potential to become the basis of a $5 billion industry. Just pop your clothes in the dryer and voilà!

Part Two

Your Extraordinary Leadership Challenge

We have formulated an extraordinary future and a business challenge. In this section, we are going to look at what it means to become an extraordinary leader who can live up to it. It has become abundantly clear that in the last decade, boards of directors gave away the keys to the kingdom to chief executives who were using the wrong leadership model. We hope to offer here in this section some ideas of what the right model for leadership might be. It is one that is based on taking a stand for an inspiring vision and empowering values that will bring out the best in those around you, will do something useful in society, and will improve the bottom line at the same time.

What Is It That Makes One Person Stand Out as a Leader?

Aircraft played a crucial role in winning World War II—but the defeat of the enemy almost resulted in the demise of the Boeing Company as well. Boeing had been a company that created bombers, and when the war ended, its revenues dropped more than 90 percent. Everyone predicted a dire future for the company—that is, with the exception of its new chief executive, Bill Allen, an unassuming attorney who had refused the job when it was first offered, saying he wasn't qualified.[1]

Allen placed a stake in the ground at one of his first meetings with employees when he said that Boeing wasn't a company that built bombers; it was a company whose designers built "extraordinary flying machines." He stated his strategic intention as early as 1952 to "transform the commercial airline industry." The first challenge involved in realizing this goal required taking the risk of investing heavily. He took a lot of heat for this when many said that Boeing was a "bomber company" and had no business being in the commercial market. People said the new chief executive didn't know what he was doing.

Allen kept up a front as a strong chief executive in public but admitted in private to being stung by the barbs; he continued to be haunted by doubts about his qualification as the company leader. Yet he remained steadfast in his commitment for a new future for Boeing. He declared publicly that it was his belief that Boeing could change the rules of the entire industry, as well as make a contribution to the national interest, which would also be in Boeing shareholders' interest.

In so doing, he went through a kind of leadership transformation, emerging as a visionary leader rather than a soft-spoken lawyer. He had reached out to the public as well as to employees with an inspiring vision and empowering values that sent the organization into high gear. Under his leadership, Boeing built not only the 707 but also 727, 737, and 747—the most successful aircraft models in commercial airline history.

At one board meeting, a board member said that if the 747 was too big a project for Boeing to take on, it could back out. Allen took a stand again: "Back out! If Boeing Aircraft Company says it will build this plane, we will build it, even if it takes all of the resources of the entire company." He remained true to this stand and became a giant in the face of it, even though he was surrounded by dwarfs who thought small—in short-term time spans, nickels per share, and with a narrow purpose.

Allen had created an extraordinary business challenge and he now needed to meet an extraordinary leadership challenge to achieve it.

The moral of the story: like Bill Allen of Boeing, a leader needs to back up an enormous business challenge with a significant leadership challenge. Allen's leadership challenge was not only taking a stand for an inspiring vision and empowering values in driving key projects such as the 747 and other planes, but also admonishing himself: "Don't talk too much. Let others talk in the face of opposition."

An example of this was when he stood before the House subcommittee in 1956 facing charges that military aircraft companies had inflated their profit margins at the expense of the taxpayer. Allen listened carefully to everything the congressmen said. Then, with no notes and no attorney whispering recommendations to plead the Fifth Amendment and no hint that he was not personally accountable for the issues that were raised, he took the floor.

When he was done speaking, no one believed that Boeing had done anything to gouge the government by beefing up executive salaries. In fact, the company had taken a stand for the future of the country by sinking profits back into research and development. The reaction of the subcommittee was beyond belief: they burst into a spontaneous standing ovation.

Declare an Extraordinary Future That Calls for Extraordinary Leadership

> *Leaders not only have a dream, they also make people believers in that dream.*

Inspiring stuff! We have asked you to declare an extraordinary future based on inspiring vision and empowering values like those of Bill Allen at Boeing. You have formulated a strategic intention and significant business challenge that represents a quantum leap for your organization. Now we are going to ask you to look at your significant leadership challenge: how you will need to develop as a leader to reach your goals.

Our stance in *Your Coach (In a Book)* is to see who you are in terms of your commitment to achieving an extraordinary future, rather than seeing you as someone who needs remedial attention. That is to say, in our eyes, you are probably a fine leader just the way you are with nothing added or taken away. At the same time, in declaring an extraordinary future for your business, you may have created a gap between who you are as a leader today and who you will need to be to bring it to pass.

Acknowledging that leadership is missing is the first step in calling forth the leadership that is needed and wanted. We'd like to ask you to think about what this gap might be, perhaps using some 360-degree feedback, as well as asking yourself, "Who do I need to be as a leader to achieve my business challenge?" Answering this question usually involves declaring what's missing that, if provided, would make a difference to who you are as a leader. It also involves shedding the winning strategies that have been the source of your success and that now are a limitation.

In our coaching work with executives we often like to say, "Let me talk to you about extraordinary leadership from the fifty-thousand-foot level, drawing on examples and making distinctions from business, government, and history rather than from the fifty-foot level where everything we say about leadership has to fit the corporate context and everyday reality."

> *A leader's vision is not limited by reality; leaders stand out in the future and create a new reality.*

For example, we once talked to John Reingold of the EMG Corporation, a Fortune 500 company, and his group. John is a highly principled, battle-hardened chief executive who had begun to make the shift to leader from administrator during a hostile takeover bid and was now ready to work with his team to create an extraordinary future.

John faced a personal leadership challenge of transforming his command-and-control approach to a more inspiring and empowering approach. He was also interested in getting through the transaction process of recent deals involved in getting a big investment bank to buy a certain class of company shares and bringing about some real change. In his own words, "There has got to be a better way to run this company."

He had asked Robert to talk to him and his group about extraordinary leadership. The talk began, "Leaders see life as much more than accumulating wealth and power and doing a series of deals. They see an opportunity to make a difference and dare to take a stand, working to bring about real change.

"Frankly," Robert continued, looking into the eyes of people in the room, "leadership often shows up as missing in corporations like this one. If we can acknowledge that leadership is missing and see that as an opportunity rather than a threat, then we can begin to call forth the leadership that is needed and wanted at EMG." As the talk began, John Nelson's hand literally started to shake; he knew Robert would say some things that would shatter the foundations of how he and others were as leaders, as well as their basic paradigms about leadership.

Robert told the group, "I want to take a stand for the next few hours in which you commit yourself to the possibility of an extraordinary future. In the context of this stand, ask yourself what will it take for you to be an extraordinary leader.

"There is a way of inquiring, of engaging in questions that can actually transform the questioner, and that is the way of inquiring that we intend to engage in here. Let's start with three questions: One, are you a leader or a power wielder? Two, do you presently show up as an ordinary transactional leader playing 'let's make a deal,' or as a transformational leader who inspires and empowers people to bring about real change? And three, what does it take for one person to transform into a leader? How would you have to *be* different, *think* different, and *act* different?"

Look in the Mirror! Are You a Leader or a Power Wielder?

As Peter Block says, leadership is a matter of putting service over self-interest.[2] Many so-called leaders in government and corporations are not leaders but power wielders. Think of political leaders: Joseph Stalin, Kim Jong-il of South Korea, Slobodan Milosevic, Saddam Hussein. And think of company leaders: "Chainsaw" Al Dunlap of Sunbeam, Kenneth Lay of Enron, and Dennis Kozlowski of Tyco. These leaders' game has been to gain, use, and retain power and, in most cases, it's been played in the pursuit of their own self-interest, with scant regard for their followers.

The scandals of the early 2000s showed chief executives with a twisted sense of ethics, living off the fat of the land with gold-plated bathrooms and company-purchased Impressionist art collections, more concerned with making money for themselves than with making a difference for the company, its employees, or its customers. The consummate example is the Enron leadership, who were dumping millions of their own company shares while telling employees to hold onto their shares to keep the price up.

Many of these so-called leaders are a lot like the emperor in the old story, the one who had no clothes. Most of them would tell you that they are exceptional leaders, but by and large they have no followers—or none less self-serving than the two tailors who sold the emperor his new suit.

In truth, over the twenty-five years we have been doing coaching, we have met few leaders whose people would walk through fire for them because they believed in who they were and what they were up to. The typical comment about company leadership adds up to something like, "They are very ambitious and only out for themselves."

> *The call to leadership is often heard by empathizing with voices of thwarted, frustrated, and pissed-off people.*

What is leadership? The fact is that leadership arises not in the mere pursuit of power and wealth but in response to real human needs and human wants. People who stand out as leaders are those who see an opportunity to make a qualitative contribution to the world and dare to take a stand. Think about Washington, Jefferson, Madison, Churchill, FDR, JFK, Martin Luther King Jr., Nelson Mandela, Mother Teresa, General Johnson (of Johnson & Johnson), and Sam Walton (of Wal-Mart).

Now think about the leaders in your company. Are they leaders or power wielders with you and others as their targets? A good question to ask yourself is, If you are a leader, where are your followers? And why are they following you?

One of the most important qualities leaders can have, whether in politics, business, health care, or in any field, is to be able to get down off their high horse and empathize with people who are in dire straights. FDR, a member of the patrician class, experienced deep compassion for the plight of the ordinary people during the Great Depression.

> *Leaders must engage followers: "I join with you, for the*
> *duration of this war." (FDR at the 1936 Democratic*
> *Convention)*

He told people during his 1936 convention address, "I join with you in meeting this great challenge of the Depression, as if we are engaged in a great war and I commit to you that we will know only victory." These four words: "I join with you" electrified the convention and engaged the people who participated as partners for Roosevelt's entire term.[3]

A good example of a chief executive whose success came from being a leader rather than a power wielder is David Packard of Hewlett-Packard (HP). He said early in his career that he wasn't interested in being a member of the chief executive club. Back in 1949, at age thirty-seven, he attended a meeting of business leaders.

Breaking into a sweat as he heard these leaders talk about how they could squeeze more profit out of their companies by always demanding more of employees, he soon erupted. He said a company had a greater responsibility than making money for its executives and shareholders. "We have a responsibility toward employees to recognize their dignity as human beings."[4]

> *Leaders must inspire followers by addressing real*
> *human needs and wants, empower them by practical*
> *solutions.*

At a time when most chief executives occupied lushly carpeted, walnut-paneled offices, Packard sat at a plain metal desk in an open workspace with the rest of his engineers. He became famous for creating the HP culture based on "management by walking around" and on giving each individual a meaningful role, making HP a very profitable company. Packard, who became a billionaire, lived in the humble house he and his wife built in 1957, and his idea of a good time was to get together with friends in Silicon Valley and string barbed wire. He also made huge donations to Stanford University, refusing in his lifetime to have any buildings named after him.

The greatest business leaders—the ones who create the greatest companies—are those like David Packard: those who have empathy for their employees, customers, and communities. They know, for example, what it is like to work in an environment where you have to jump through a lot of hierarchal and bureaucratic hoops to get anything done, and they protect their employees from that fate.

What have you done to make the world a better place lately?

They know what it is like to go on a business trip in a cramped economy seat on a transatlantic flight where there is no room for your knees, or how it is to stay in a hotel room in Prague and not be able to get the news because you don't speak Czech, or to call home because your cell phone doesn't work overseas. Such leaders hear the call to leadership—the human needs and human wants of their employees and customers. As a result, they take a stand to provide what is missing that can make a difference.

Jack Welch had a personal hatred of hierarchy and bureaucracy for its stultifying effects on people and thereby took his organization through "Work-Out" sessions designed to get the people talking to their bosses. Ted Turner came up with twenty-four-hour cable news available in English to anyone almost anywhere around the globe. Richard Branson came up with the idea of the super economy transoceanic airline seat, big enough for your knees and for not much more than $1500, rather than $8000 for business class.

Are You a Transformational or Transactional Leader?

Frank Tomey, a leader at General Electric (GE) with a business the size of a Fortune 500 company, told Robert his business challenge (which actually came down from GE's new CEO, Jeff Immelt) was to dramatically grow his business with a yearly goal of a 10 percent increase in growth and a 20 percent ROCE (return on capital employed).

He said that reaching this goal would not only require some bold business moves but also a passionate organization where *edge*, the ability to make tough yes/no decisions (something that existed today) was balanced with *compassion* or caring about people. He said, in order to do this, his leadership challenge was to transform himself from a "deal maker" to a "leader."

Robert Writes . . .

In 2003 I had the opportunity to attend a Renaissance Weekend with two hundred fascinating people. Guests in former years had included three U.S. presidents; this Renaissance Weekend included U.S. Senators, army generals, a Nobel Prize winner in physics, chief executives of big companies, ambassadors, architects, artists, educators, doctors, students, and others.

After holding a session on the topic, "Insights from a Masterful Coach," I walked out of the conference room to a patio area and saw an elderly gentleman with "extreme gravitas" reading the *New York Times*. The name on his badge rang a bell, so I walked over to a table where he was sitting and said politely, "Are you *the* James MacGregor Burns that wrote about the difference between 'transactional' and 'transformational' leadership?" Burns smiled and said, "I am," which triggered a stimulating, engaging, and profound conversation about leadership that spanned the far reaches of human history, political science, government, and business.[5]

> *Do you have track record of making a difference in your world by bringing about irreversible change?*

I found Burns's use of historical examples of people like Washington, Jefferson, Lincoln, and FDR refreshing. So many business articles are written as if the only leaders in the world are Jack Welch, Andrew Grove, Bill Gates, and Warren Buffett.

Transactional Leaders Practice the Art of the Deal

According to Burns, *transactional* leadership is the ordinary, day-in, day-out kind practiced in all organizations. Says Burns, "Transactional leadership involves negotiating, deal making, and brokering." For example, a U.S. president may say that if you vote to pass my defense project, I will lobby for a new shipyard to be located in your state.

A transactional CEO might approach another for a merger deal and point out that it has a $20 million golden parachute pay-off for both. Likewise, an executive might tell a transactional direct report, "I need you to take on the job of cleaning up XYZ division," and receive the answer, "If I do that for you, what will you do for me?" You achieve small changes in your world by striking deals, and they may well be beneficial. The acid test, according to Burns, is what good comes from all these transactions.

One leader with excellent transactional skills is retired chairman Sandy Weil, who merged Citibank and Travelers and created the biggest financial services company in today's world. Yet most would argue that the combined bank is merely bigger, not better. Transactional leaders may have a certain genius, but they come and go in most organizations, replaced by other transactional leaders. If you look for the legacy that a departed transactional leader has left, it is often difficult to find.

On a day-in, day-out basis, transactional leadership is practiced in every organization and involves the normal performance contracts, backed up by carrots and sticks: "Meet these goals and we will reward you with a 10 percent increase in pay and perhaps, if you are lucky, a promotion." Such leadership falls short of getting people to give their emotional commitment to something, but is effective to some degree in getting compliance. It is said that, even though people are paid a lot to do a good job, the best work is often done by volunteers. When people are giving their emotional commitment, you will usually find that it has do with transformational leadership and the principles behind it.

Transformational Leaders Bring About Fundamental Change

Transformational leaders are extraordinary leaders who have been touched by an inspiring vision and empowering values. They see an opportunity to make a difference and dare to take a stand. They engage people by speaking and listening in a way that frames human grievances, needs, and wants. They empower people by touching them with new possibilities and converting these to bold and unreasonable action. As a result, they mobilize people to bring about the introduction of a new order of things.

Burns pointed out that human history offers many examples of transformational leaders, yet none better than the founding fathers of the United States: Washington, Jefferson, and Madison. They were steeped in the empowering ideas of the philosophies of the eighteenth-century Enlightenment: the right to life, liberty, and the pursuit of happiness. They saw an opportunity to make a difference against the hand of tyranny and took a stand by signing the Declaration of Independence. The Declaration was one of the most powerful calls to leadership in history.

Transformational leaders often inspire followers through a higher vision or purpose to choose service over self-interest. One of my favorite examples of transformational leadership is Admiral Horatio Nelson, who—outgunned by Napoleon's ships ten to one at the Battle of Trafalgar—won the day by brilliantly positioning his ships and inspiring his men about the importance of defeating the despot Napoleon, even though many lives would be lost. Nelson was known for treating common seamen with a great deal of personal consideration.

Other examples of transformational leaders include such charismatic leaders as Abraham Lincoln, Mao Tse Tung, Mahatma Gandhi, FDR, JFK, Nelson Mandela, and Martin Luther King Jr. The acid test of transformational leaders, however, is not their charisma or other leadership traits, but that they bring about a profound change.

It is important to point out the difference between transformation and change. Change represents replacing one thing with another. Transformation represents an alteration of substance. A transformation occurs when a caterpillar turns into a butterfly, a despotic government into a democratic society, a buggy whip plant into an auto assembly line.

As to the leaders we cite as examples, each brought about a transformation by standing for an idea that had transformational potential. Lincoln freed the slaves, Mao transformed China from a feudal society to a modern one with a future, FDR ended the Great Depression and put his stamp on the U.S. government for decades, Nelson Mandela almost single-handedly put an end to apartheid.

You achieve major changes in the world by standing for
an idea that has transformational potential.

Business offers many examples of transformational leaders who stood for the kind of inspiring vision and empowering values that result in a great enterprise, and who made a difference both in their organization and in the world around them. Think back to 1981, the year that Chrysler almost went into bankruptcy. Lee Iacocca soon became a national icon, author of a best-selling book, star of hundreds of TV commercials, and everyone's image of an ideal chief executive who turned around his company's sinking fortunes.

The same year, the stock of Fannie Mae also hit the skids and a different kind of chief executive was hired to save the shaken mortgage lender. This man, David Maxwell, never became a national hero like Lee Iacocca, nor even a name that most people have recognized in his prime, let alone today. Yet by the time both men hung up their skates and retired, Maxwell had increased the value of his stock at a rate more than double what Iacocca achieved for Chrysler.

It is said that Maxwell was inspired yet not inspiring, and more deliberative than dazzling. "He took a burning house and not only saved it, but also turned it into a cathedral." Some of his moves, such as selling off $10 billion in unprofitable mortgages, were classic transactional stuff. Yet his brilliance was in reframing the company around a mission: "Strengthening America's social fabric by democratizing home ownership."[6]

He reasoned that if Fannie Mae were able to deliver on this mission, people traditionally excluded from the American dream of home ownership—single-parent families, minorities, and immigrants—could easily discover the satisfaction of living under a roof that they owned. If leadership is an art, then Maxwell is a master painter. Under his direction the company not only became highly successful but allowed millions to claim their stake in the American dream.

Great Leaders Have Both Transformational and Transactional Skills

Now that we have framed *transformational* and *transactional leadership*, let's be clear that, while we have been talking about what may sound like two incompatible types of leadership, the most success-ful leaders seem to have some combination of both orientations, and the lack of either can be limiting. Mao and Gandhi were both transformational leaders with limited transactional skills, which made their approach more confrontational than collaborative and limited what they could achieve to some degree.

Roosevelt had both skill sets. First of all Roosevelt was not afraid to take a stand. As Burns says, who could forget his speech at Madison Square Garden to an aroused crowd in the midst of the Depression, with opposition swirling around him from big busi-ness, the Republicans, and the Supreme Court?

"Government by organized money is just as much a tyranny as government by an organized mob. Never before have so many stood together in hatred of a candidate. Let me tell you, I welcome their hatred." Roosevelt not only enacted a great deal of transfor-mational legislation, he was constantly wheeling and dealing with Congress and the courts to get it passed on a transactional basis.

Transformational leaders must pass three acid tests:

- Have a high vision and principles that mobilize followers to bring about the introduction of a new order of things.
- Bring about a lasting transformational change that makes a difference in their world.
- Create a climate or environment that brings out the best in those around them.

Meanwhile, transactional leaders must pass a separate set of tests:

- Create a powerful agenda and identify partnerships needed to achieve it.
- Build coalitions based on interests, not positions.
- Make deals effectively. This could involve back-and-forth negotiating to pull off a big merger or to get buy-in on a trans-formational process change, or the day-in, day-out brokering and contracting required to make something happen among diverse people and departments in a large project. (See Figure Part 2.1.)

**Figure Part 2.1. Leadership Requires Both
Transformational and Transactional Leadership Skills.**

Transformational Leadership

- Requires high vision and principles that mobilize followers to introduce a new order of things.
- Brings about a lasting transformational change that makes a difference in their world.
- Creates a climate or environment that brings out the best in everyone involved.

Transactional Leadership

- Creates a powerful agenda and identifies partnerships needed to achieve it.
- Builds coalitions based on interests, not positions.
- Makes deals effectively.

What Does It Take to Transform into a Leader?

It is our experience that thousands of people possess the innate gift of leadership but never discover or express it because they look for it in the wrong places. They study leadership characteristics and traits, hoping to somehow get these leadership qualities into themselves by understanding them well enough to absorb them.

This attempt produces lots of information and little impact on anyone's leadership ability. In fact, the ability to discover and express your own leadership ability comes about as a result of you as an individual recognizing the opportunity to make a difference and taking a stand. The classic example is Rosa Parks, the civil rights leader who refused to move to the back of the bus.

What does it take to actually transform one person into a leader? Most people ask the question, "Are leaders born or made?" We reply that the answer is both. Certain people do seem to naturally possess leadership ability, the ability to be agents of change.

However, these people are often only able to call themselves forth as leaders when faced with a "change ready" situation that becomes an alchemical cauldron for leadership transformation. People like Abraham Lincoln in the dark days of the Civil War, FDR in the middle of the Depression, JFK during the Cuban Missile crisis are examples of this.

Leaders follow their passion and infect others with it.
Their postscript is to leave a legacy.

An excellent business example of how inspiring leadership often emerges as a result a change-ready situation and dares to take a stand is James Burke of Johnson & Johnson. If you ask people to tell you the single most important act of CEO courage that they can think of, many will still reply by citing Burke's decision to pull all Tylenol off the shelves in 1981 after discovering that a few bottles had been tainted with poison, a decision that cost the company hundreds of millions.

His leadership challenge came when he gathered twenty executives in a room and banged his fist on a copy of the Johnson & Johnson credo. Written by General Johnson in 1943, it said, "We believe our first responsibility is to the doctors, nurses and patients, to mothers and fathers and all others who use our products and services." As the twenty executives in the room fretted and bit pencils wondering what to do about the Tylenol crisis, Burke told them, "Here is the credo, we are either going to live by it or tear it off the wall." The group rallied behind him. Up until this time Burke had been thought of as an able administrator, but in the twinkling of an eye, his words caused the group to rally behind him and he was transformed into a leader.[7]

Formulating Your Leadership Challenge

Let's get back to you. Are you ready to formulate your leadership challenge based on everything we have said here? In this work, it is more important to pay attention to what you can declare as possible for yourself than to pay attention to your present job title, situation, or even the historical evidence. Answer the following questions, keeping in mind the principle, "Get it so that it is 80 percent right, then go back to it after a rest."

- In order to reach my [company] business challenge of: _____
- I am committed to the possibility of [describe the leader you intend to be]: _____
- I am committed to giving up [outdated winning strategies and other dysfunctional behavior]: _____

- The transformational leadership skills I need to develop are:

  _____

- The transactional leadership skills I need to develop are:

  _____

- From this point on, I will draw my identity as a leader from my commitment; the stand that I am taking here is:

  _____

The Chapters of This Section

Once you have articulated your leadership challenge, and have resolved to become a new kind of leader, you will be ready to read the next section of *Your Coach (In a Book)*. You will learn to expand yourself beyond old strategies that may now be limiting you. You will learn how to take a stand and speak, listen, and act in a way that matters on a day-in, day-out basis. Then you will learn how to get what you are standing for "over the line" so that it begins to exist independent of you. You will discover that to make the difference you want to make, you need to master the corporate chessboard as well as build successful coalitions. You will also learn how to create a team of passionate, talented "A" players. Finally, you will learn how to leverage your personal effectiveness by managing your focus, not your time, as well as by preparing for key meetings so that you can bring home a big win.

Chapter 9

Be an Extraordinary Leader

Recognize That Your Winning Strategy
has Gotten You Here But May Not
Take You Where You Want to Go

 SITUATION: The ways of being and thinking, the attitudes that were the source of your success in the past, have now become the source of your limitations. You're unaware of this, and you are unaware that you are unaware. *Your masterful coach will rip the blinders off.*

Michel in a Coaching Conversation with a Vice President of an Industrial Firm

Lars Jeffords, the six-foot-two, bearlike vice president of United Signal Manufacturing, a major industrial firm, has just received word that he has a shot at becoming chief executive of his company, if he can be less of a *reactionary* manager and more of a *visionary* leader. This would mean becoming a leader who creates an Impossible Future by coming up with new wealth-creating strategies that rally the organization, rather than being a leader who attempts to wring more costs out of the system, often at the expense of chewing people up and spitting them out.

The chief executive of United told me in the 360-degree feedback interview that Lars had tremendous natural leadership skills, but something was holding him back from discovering and expressing them. He explained that a couple of years ago, when the production business was in trouble, he'd told Lars, "You either turn that business around or we will have to take drastic action." Lars responded by selling off some assets and cutting the cost out of others. He was promoted as a result, and ever since he has tended to default to the same cost-cutting approach in every situation.

I met with Lars one afternoon in the company dining room and gave him this feedback. Extending him the same high value on his leadership potential that his boss gave him, I explained that he had a *winning strategy* that had led him to be successful but was now potentially limiting him from getting to the top. He asked, "What do you mean, winning strategy?"

I said, "Look at it this way, Lars. A number of years ago in your career as a leader and manager you faced a hurdle. To get over that hurdle, you figured out a success strategy and it worked very well—fix something, close something, sell something. The feedback says that you have been using that same success strategy ever since. The point is that today you are facing a different kind of hurdle and using that strategy won't get you over it, no matter how sincerely or intelligently you try.

"To get over *this* hurdle, you have to start thinking in terms of the chief executive as a visionary who creates an Impossible Future rather than as a profit mechanic, as an entrepreneur who creates innovative business concepts instead of as a steward who polishes up grandma's china (hard assets), and as an emotional leader rather than as an administrator. If you are willing to commit yourself to that kind of transformation over the next year to eighteen months, I think there is nothing stopping you from getting to the CEO's office. I know this sounds like a tall order, but your boss has told me that you have brought out these leadership qualities at earlier points in your career. So now it's a matter of calling them forth into your present situation, while at the same time letting up on your winning strategy a bit."

◆ ◆ ◆

I was packing my clothes for a business trip when the phone rang. "Hello, Michel. Doug Holt here. Are you available to speak right now? I would like your thoughts on something that is been bugging me." Doug is only thirty-three years old and already occupies a high-impact position as the lead strategist for the Gillette Marketing Organization. Short for time, I respond, "I have thirty minutes to give you. Let's get to the heart of the matter."

"Okay, here is my issue. I was hired as a strategist directly out of Sloan School of Business, where I earned top marks. I have spent the last nine years in various strategy positions and I have earned a reputation for being good at it. However, I am concerned that I am putting myself in a box and that, as a result, I will end up doing strategy work for the next thirty years."

I told Doug that his boss, Carl Haden, had said he was indeed a brilliant strategic thinker. "Well, that is exactly my issue. My boss and others see me as a strategist and seem to have no intention to train me for a top management position. The truth is that what I aspired to is a senior leadership position in the company. Michel, I love working with people, I love a challenge, and I want to get ahead in my career. I would love running a large part of the organization. At the same time, I must admit I have not been helping my own cause. I have been shying away from pursuing opportunities where my leadership skills would be tested. I do not always feel confident, so I revert to safer challenges."

"Ah ha! Stop right there, Doug! What you just said is key. What you are talking about is what we call your *winning strategy*, and how responsible you are for its impact on others' listening. Your winning strategy is the unique way you have developed to maximize winning and to avoid losing. It defines who you are in your own eyes and in the eyes of others. It includes a distinct set of skills you have developed and a whole set of conditioned responses to any situation.

"The bottom line, Doug, is that it is time to free yourself up from your winning strategy so you can take on bigger and better challenges. From what your boss tells me, you have the potential to be a full-fledged business leader—much more than a staffer in charge of strategy. Making the shift starts with declaring new possibilities for yourself, like being a leader of a business unit with profit-and-loss responsibilities. On top of this, just imagine how the strategist skills you have will be an asset for the leadership roles you take on. Now it is also time to expand other skills and determine a challenge that will propel you forward."

"Michel, I hear you and I am ready."

TEACHABLE POINT OF VIEW: Recognize that the winning strategy that made you successful in the past may be the limitation to creating a new future.

Just like your organization, you also have a winning strategy. Your winning strategy can be defined as the set of strategies and skilled behaviors that are the source of your success and also the source of your current limitations. A typical example of this is the chief executive who pulls off great deals (transactions), but never brings about transformational change in the organization. Or it could be a business leader like Lars, who tries to shrink the way to greatness by cutting costs but never does anything to grow the business.

People don't just have a winning strategy; they *become* their winning strategy. They draw their identity from it because their winning strategy is the source of the results they currently enjoy. At the same time, however successful they have been with it, that winning strategy inevitably becomes a limit to who they are as leaders and to what is possible for them to accomplish.

Your winning strategy is the particular combination of positive and productive traits, skills, and competencies you employ as your standard response in any situation. For example, being a visionary leader, taking charge of change, thinking outside the box, or driving for results. Your winning strategy can also include negative or unproductive behaviors that you are unaware of, such as creating pie-in-the-sky goals, dominating others with your views, jumping into action without sufficient thought, or delivering results with a last-minute scramble. These represent "skilled incompetence"— skilled behaviors that lead to unintended results.

When you become your winning strategy, you have no choice but to respond as your winning strategy dictates. It becomes not just your strong suit but your default position and is your standard response to all situations, even if inappropriate and ineffective. The problem is that your strategy for success becomes a self-imposed limitation—a straitjacket from which it is hard to escape. Who you are and what is possible for you becomes rather narrowly defined in terms of your winning strategy, both in your own mind and in the imaginations of others throughout the organization.

In most cases, when people declare a business challenge that represents an Impossible Future, it also requires them to take on a leadership challenge that represents going to the next level. The challenge is first to expand your sense of yourself, which requires that you jettison your winning strategy to some degree. Your winning strategy needs to become one of a variety of ways you have of acting or responding in any given situation, depending on the requirements of the moment, instead of the predictable, default response. In addition, it is equally important to engage intentionally in conversations and activities that will help other people throughout the organization to see you in the light of new and enlarged possibilities.

TEMPLATE FOR ACTION

1. *Define your winning strategy.* Write down what you think your winning strategy is. Engage in a conscious inquiry with yourself to uncover all aspects of your winning strategy— good or bad. Ask yourself the following questions, and tell yourself the truth about the answers:

What skills have I developed of which I am most proud?
What practices do I have that have contributed to my success?
What behaviors do I have that work (for example: good listener, great at pep talks, likable) and those that don't work (for example: last-minute panic, jumping into action too quickly)?

What are my predictable patterns of response when confronted with a new challenge?

How do I think others perceive me?

Do I avoid certain challenges or areas where I would like to aspire but don't feel I am able?

What are the limitations of my current winning strategy?

2. *Engage others in your inquiry.* Let other people know the path you are on—that you would like to grow as a leader and incorporate new skills and behaviors. Ask them to be frank with you about how they perceive you, what they consider to be your strengths, weaknesses, and limitations. You may want to ask them the questions you asked of yourself in item 1. Ask both professional and personal acquaintances. Avoid being offended or defensive about the answers you get, so as to create an environment where people will tell you the truth.

3. *Define and commit yourself to new areas of growth and skills that require stepping outside your winning strategy.* What is next for you as a leader? To what kind of role do you aspire? Identify the skills, practices, and behaviors you will need to learn to move forward in your career (and life).

4. *Create a business challenge that will pull you toward a leadership transformation.* Stand in your commitment to the business and look at your current role through new eyes. Identify a project or challenge about which you can be passionate—an initiative that will both make a critical difference to your department or company as a whole and require that you call forth a new level of leadership in order to deliver, that will push you outside the comfort zone of your winning strategy. An example for Doug Holt (the strategy guy mentioned earlier in this chapter) might be, "I will lead an organization-wide, relentless implementation of our new strategy and business model, and make this implementation the fuel that drives us to be the most successful marketing business in the United States."

5. *Declare who you will be as a leader.* Stand in the business challenge you have created and formulate a leadership challenge that addresses the questions of who you will need to be to succeed with the commitment and, at the same time, to fulfill the vision you have of yourself for your career. Write an overall commitment statement that summarizes your leadership transformation and supply that with a list of

specific behaviors and new practices. For example, David might write: "I will make sure that leaders at all levels own the vision, the strategy, and the new business model and contribute to its implementation." And then the specifics: "I will be a leader who gets out of the confines of the office to spend more time in conversations with people, communicates the vision and strategy relentlessly to teams and individuals, challenges and coaches people to raise their game, embraces communication upward, and is not a victim of a winning strategy."

6. *Create an environment of support and commitment.* Invite others to relate to you in the light of the new possibility you have created for yourself. Meet with your boss and share your insights into your winning strategy and its limitations, and your commitment to grow as a leader. Ask for your boss's commitment to your success and the fulfillment of your business and leadership challenges in the form of coaching and providing feedback. Share your commitments with your direct reports and engage them as thinking partners from time to time. Pick a couple of direct reports with whom you are comfortable and seek regular feedback on your progress as a leader and suggestions on how you can do better.

7. *Find a coach or a mentor who is committed to your success and has the skills you wish to develop.* Once you have engaged this kind of support, meet regularly. Let your coach know your progress, your challenges, your insecurities. Your coach has probably personally encountered them all, and can offer valuable insights, encouragement, and advice. More than this, however, find a role model. We are often altered simply by being in the presence of someone who possesses the skills to which we aspire and who is generous with that fund of personal experience.

8. *Keep your boss and your reports (and anyone else who can make a difference in the organizational "conversation") informed.* Sometimes people can, for any number of reasons, get stuck in an old perspective on you and need a little nudge to recognize new patterns of growth and accomplishment. Your job is to keep shining a light in the direction of the new set of possibilities you are creating for yourself.

Chapter 10

Stand for Something!

Leadership Arises in Discovering Yourself as the Stand You Take

 SITUATION: You have declared an impossible future and taken on a powerful business challenge, but sense you now need to take on an equally powerful leadership challenge that will require relentless coaching and feedback. *If you are ready to develop faster, fasten your seat belt and let's go.*

Michel in a Coaching Conversation with a Telecommunications Company Leader

I am sitting at Milos, a celebrated Greek restaurant in Montreal, across from Claudio Bongiorno, dapper in Armani business casual, who is ordering a bottle of wine. Claudio is charming, elegant, and quietly powerful. Formerly CEO of Coca-Cola Italy, he is now president of Telco Communications North America, a network services company, and has been a client for six months. Normally I would be studying the menu, eagerly anticipating a feast of calamari salad, broiled scallops the size of a fist, and five-pound Nova Scotia lobster. Yet my thoughts are not on the coming meal but on the tough conversation I will have to have with Claudio.

Four months earlier, Claudio had taken a powerful stand to lead his organization to a new future. I remember his energy and passion as he declared, "I am committed to making Telco Communications the number one market leader in North America. We are the underdog in a pack of four, with the smallest resources. We will achieve dominance by changing the rules of competitive engagement and by exceeding customer expectations and leveraging our new network technology. It is my belief that, if we act consistent with our stand, we will reach our goal in three years."

I was inspired by the commitment and courage of Claudio's stand, especially by the fact that he declared his commitment to be market leader in the press, which made it nonnegotiable. I also noticed that, in the weeks following this declaration, Claudio seemed to go through a remarkable leadership transformation. He was now emerging as a visionary leader, operating in the domain of risk, taking bold action rather than showing up in his old mode, as an administrator with a tendency to micromanage and avoid confrontation. Rather than needing to have all the answers, he began to draw on others' expertise and strength to find solutions to tough issues.

During the course of a few coaching calls, however, I began to wonder if Claudio's old winning formula was beginning to creep in. One call raised a red flag when Claudio made excuses for not getting around to addressing some very tough issues with his group about the way they were working together. Then he canceled a regularly scheduled meeting with his team to evaluate where they were in terms of vision milestones, which might have required cutting costs. I also heard that some of Claudio's direct reports were backstabbing him, and rather than confronting it, he seemed to be hiding in his office studying matrices, typing e-mail, sending out recommendations.

So as we met that evening at Milos, I knew I needed to challenge Claudio to take a stand for who he needed to be as a leader, to declare and commit to a whole new possibility for himself in the domain of leadership. I wasted no time in throwing my first salvo. "Claudio," I said, "you are falling back into old habits; you are reverting to the comfort of your winning strategy—you know, the way you have always managed to win in previous jobs. Yet being who you have been in the past is insufficient in leading your organization to the future you have declared." I went on to give some examples.

"Michel, yes, it's fair to say that lately I have reverted to old habits." He paused and went on, "I lost it, I guess."

"Okay, Claudio. Let's formulate a leadership declaration for who you will be from now on, in service of your vision. With this declaration, we will create a whole new possibility for you as a leader." I wrote some questions down on a napkin, slid it across the table, and asked Claudio to fill in the blanks. He looked at the napkin, smiled, wrote something down, and then read what he wrote, "I am committed to the possibility of being a leader who not only takes a stand that a difference can be made, but speaks and listens from that stand, rigorously following through in action. I am committed to giving up always needing to look good and avoiding conflict, always needing to have all the answers, and micromanaging."

I worked intensively with Claudio on both his leadership and his business challenge over the next year and a half. One day I picked up a copy of the *Globe and Mail:* "Claudio Bongiorno has announced that Telco Communications North America has reached its goal of becoming the Number 1 Market Leader and now reveals his ambitious plans for the future." I called Claudio to congratulate him. "That's terrific," I said. "Your leadership brought your strategic intention over the line."

"Your coaching made a big difference, Michel. Thank you."

TEACHABLE POINT OF VIEW: Leadership arises in discovering yourself as the stand that you take.

Taking a stand often involves embracing a possibility or level of responsibility larger than oneself and is a transformational opportunity.

The call to leadership involves seeing an opportunity to make a difference and daring to take a stand. Taking a stand is the most powerful act available to us as human beings to change the face of things. By its very nature, taking a stand is imbued with vision. It lives in the possibility of a new future, one that will make a difference to people and mobilize them to bring about change. It is our observation that leadership arises in taking a stand at the moment when you are called to be someone you have not been before. Once you have taken a stand for something you consider important, you must then call forth in yourself the courage to live consistent with your commitment on a daily basis. Let's take an example.

On August 3, 1963, Katherine Graham heard the crack of a gunshot inside her home. She ran down the stairs to discover that her husband, Phillip, lay dead, having taken his own life. On top of her shock and sadness, she had another weight on her chest, responsibility for the *Washington Post*. What would happen to it now? The next day she told the board she would not sell the company, but would act as its steward. Graham, who says in her memoirs that she "suffered from life long insecurity," went way beyond herself and the concept of stewardship in fulfilling her new role.[1]

You learn to draw your identity from the bold new future you are standing for, rather than from your history.

At the time, the *Washington Post* was an unacclaimed regional newspaper. Graham created the strategic intent that people throughout the country would speak of it at the same level as the *New York Times*. A turning point came in 1971 when she had to look in the mirror and decide what to do with the Pentagon Papers (a leaked document that was highly controversial concerning the Vietnam War). The *Times* was already facing a court injunction for publishing excerpts from the document. If the *Post* went to press with the Pentagon Papers, it risked being taken to court under the Espionage Act.

> *You begin to stand out as a leader as you speak, listen,*
> *and act from your stand.*

This could immediately harm the *Post*'s chances of getting a public stock offering and TV license approved. Graham realized she would be risking the whole company on her decision. To opt for assured survival at the cost of the company would be worse than not surviving. The *Post* went to press with the Pentagon Papers, and was eventually vindicated by a Supreme Court decision. This was a remarkable decision for an accidental CEO whose memoirs are laced with phrases like "I was terrified," or "I was shaking in my boots." This anxiety would return when reporters Woodward and Bernstein presented her with the opportunity to publish the story known as "Watergate," which eventually brought down a president.

> *At the end of the day, the person who was there before is*
> *not there now. The person that exists now was not there*
> *before.*

To us Katherine Graham's story is a great example of the fact that the call to leadership often begins with recognizing an opportunity to make a difference and daring to take a stand. Graham repeatedly claims little credit for herself in her memoirs, saying she had no choice on these decisions. The fact is that she did have a choice, and she took a stand, not only based on an empowering vision and values for the *Post*, but also for the value of personal integrity in a leader.

TEMPLATE FOR ACTION

1. *Declare your greater vision and commitment to the organization.* Examine your business (or area of the business) and identify the unique opportunity you have to leave a lasting legacy, to truly make a difference. What do you stand for? What new reality or future will you bring into existence? What will you hold yourself accountable for? Commit boldly and publicly to the future you have chosen. Act immediately from your commitment to the new future.

2. *Declare a new possibility for who you will be as a leader.* Declare who you need to be as a leader in service of the future to which you have committed. When you commit to a compelling new future, who you are today and what you have done so far as a leader is probably insufficient to the challenge in front of you. Formulate a new possibility for who you are as a leader, declare the new possibility and commit to it! This is your leadership declaration.

3. *Identify old patterns and behaviors that will get in the way.* Your winning strategy got you where you are today. You will tend to revert to it, especially in times of great tension. You have years of practice with these behaviors. Don't underestimate the hold they have on you. Identify three or four of your leadership behaviors or patterns that will be counterproductive as you go forward—that will get in the way of achieving your vision. Then formulate three or four statements of commitment that describe how you will transform as a leader. These specifics will put flesh to your leadership declaration.

4. *Declare your stand publicly.* Identify the people who will play a role in making your business and leadership commitments a reality. Share your commitment with them. Speak with power. Enlist their support. Enroll people, day in and day out. Identify a few people that work with you or for you, people you trust, and invite them to be committed listeners for your leadership declaration. Ask them to give you honest feedback on a regular basis. Be coachable.

5. *Find internal resources for your stand, day in and day out.* Get into action. It is predictable that you will from time to time forget and stop being your stand. You might get in a reactive mode, or get overwhelmed with details. You might encounter setbacks that throw you off or you might allow your old cruise control to turn itself on. To successfully deliver on the future you have declared, you will need to keep the times when you are not standing powerfully in your commitment as brief as possible. To do that, every week (or even every day) review your written commitment statement and ask yourself, What can I do today to forward the action, to truly make a difference? When you notice that you are off, take the time to call yourself forth to stand newly in your commitment.

6. *Be ready to live with the tension of what is missing.* Recognize the gap created by your declaration. As soon as you declare a new future, you immediately create a natural tension between the current reality

and your vision of the future. All the things that are missing will now show up. A leader who stands for something needs to welcome the resulting tension. Furthermore, a leader needs to accept personal responsibility for identifying what is missing and ensuring that what is missing gets provided.

Chapter 11

Get Your Grand Design Over the Line

Vision Is Not Enough! Execute on Your Source Document Until It Exists Independent of You

SITUATION: You spent three months working on your Source Document as if you were writing your enterprise's version of the U.S. Constitution. You put out your vision, teachable points of view, and key priorities at town hall meetings with a bang, but what has come back is more like a whimper. *We'll show you how to get what you are committed to "over the line" so that it exists independent of you.*

Michel in a Coaching Conversation with a Nonprofit Leader

It was a long, hot afternoon in Toronto that seemed to make even the tall steel and glass buildings of the city droop with the weight of the humidity and absence of even the faintest breeze. Julia Peters arrived in the restaurant with her coiffed red hair turned up sharply at one edge. Her impeccable business suit had not the slightest hint of a wrinkle. I had been coaching Julia, a former Wall Street executive now serving as director of an international nonprofit with a great cause, for eight months.

Julia sat down at the table and I asked her how it was going. "Michel, I just don't know. We spent our first few months together working on the Source Document. I was totally inspired by the vision, the goals, and our teachable points of views. I spoke passionately about these in all our town hall meetings. Everyone seemed to buy into it, but Michel, I have to tell you," she said, leaning back and shaking her head, "I am at my wits' end. Something is really wrong. The team seems to have embraced the vision and say they don't disagree with any of the teachable points of view, however, that's as far as it goes. If I were to leave today, the whole thing would disappear."

"Julia," I said, "I am going to tell you something that you probably won't like to hear. You have totally underestimated the reality of what it will take to alter the prevailing attitudes or thinking in your organization or, as I like to say, to 'source' your organization. It is going to take tremendous courage and commitment on your part as a leader to get your grand design outlined in your Source Document over the line."

Julia looked a bit crushed, so I stepped back a bit, "Okay, you've done the first two steps. You created the Source Document and communicated it through the town hall meetings, and let me congratulate you for that. At the same time, you assumed that communicating it once would be enough to get people to march to the beat of your drum. To get your Source Document over the line, you not only have to be an architect who comes up with the grand design but also a master builder who brings it into existence. This means focusing on your inspiring vision and empowering values. It also means putting the superstructures that you will need in place—specific goals and major milestones—that create line of sight to your dream. You have to lay in the key initiatives like major building blocks of your grand design."

"Michel, I get it; let's go!"

TEACHABLE POINT OF VIEW: Vision isn't enough! Execute on your Source Document until it exists independent of you.

It is not enough to have an ideology. You have to infect people with it.

A vision doesn't just happen. It needs to be powerfully sourced. It is a job that can't be delegated. The job of sourcing is only partly about formulating your vision (all the stuff in your Source Document); the major factor is execution, or as we like to say, "getting your grand design over the line." In our estimation, great leaders spend about 70 percent of their time executing on or building out their grand design in a new leadership job, and 30 percent of their time in a job on it when they have been in place for a while. The goal is to make your vision, goals, and teachable point of view exist independent of you so that you leave a lasting legacy to your organization. Here is an example of someone who achieved this.

Few people have even heard of Charles Coffin, but this remarkable man was followed by many great leaders. He was the founding entrepreneur of a company that held the patents to the electric light, the phonograph, the motion picture, and so on. Coffin understood his role was not to be the next Edison, but rather be an inventor of a different sort. His creation was the General Electric Company (GE).[1]

Between 1892 and 1912, Coffin established a tradition of developing general managers with the view to steadily increasing profits per executive. In so doing, he created a machine that generated a succession of giants. While Coffin was followed by many great leaders, the likes of Cordiner and Jones, GE eventually became known as the "House That Jack Built." In reality, Jack Welch was a product of GE, not its source.

Yet at the same time, Welch recreated Coffin's vision by adopting the founder's teachable point of view, frequently referring to GE as a "People Factory." Welch not only showed up at the Crotonville Leadership Center countless times, he also got personally involved in improving on GE's people development processes. At the same time, when Welch (considered by many to be North America's greatest executive) left the company, he didn't have to worry that people would forget to do these things.

Think of yourself as not just a visionary but a chief
architect and master builder with your sleeves rolled up.

The new CEO, Jeff Immelt, who took the helm in 2002—a century after the midpoint of Coffin's tenure—continued in the tradition of GE's founder.[2] "We run the company so people feel the CEO might enter their world anytime. I spend roughly 40 percent of my time on people issues; so do our other top leaders." Immelt sees Coffin and Welch not only as visionaries but also as chief architect and master builder of the GE "People Factory." His role is to take it to the next level.

"I teach at Crotonville three to four times a month. I will review in detail 5000 to 6000 resumes in a process we call 'Session C.' I am not locked in a room with executives. I reach down hard into the organization all the time. I will spend time in the field with sales reps identified as high potential. When I meet people I am impressed with, I call human resources right away and say, for example, 'I want these three people to get a double dip of stock options.'" One of the most interesting things to us about what Coffin did at GE theater, even though almost no one remembers his name today, "He built the stage on which they all played."

TEMPLATE FOR ACTION

1. *Tell yourself, "If it is to be, it's up to me."* Imagine for a moment that you are taking over from a very strong leader—the Thomas Edison of your company, for example, or even a lesser notable. You have re-imagined the future and put it in your Source Document, which gives you a place to stand.

Now you have to keep reminding yourself that it's up to you. Use every conversation to refer back to the inspiring vision and empowering values in your Source Document. Next figure out the most important things to focus on—whether it's creating a "people factory," "new growth engines," or "unforgettable customer experiences"—and don't delegate any of them to anyone until it takes on a life of its own. Make sure your own personal attitudes and behavior personify everything in your Source Document. If they don't, it's all over.

2. *Put out your vision, goals, and teachable point of view with every breath.* Your job is to communicate the Grand Design until it becomes the vision, climate, and spirit of the company. Richard Branson has a set of governing values for any new Virgin business, which he constantly talks about: have the best quality, provide great value, be innovative, dramatically challenge existing alternatives, and provide a sense of fun or "cheekiness." Leaders are people who land the vision and teachable point of view one conversation at a time by defining a new reality, asking people to re-imagine whatever they are doing, giving their absolute best. For example, the great ballet choreographer Sergei Diaghilev routinely implored ballerinas, "Astonish me!" Nintendo's former chief executive, Hiroshi Yamauchi, when asked by the company's top game designer what he should do next, answered, "Build something great!" A copywriter once asked advertising legend David Ogilvy what he expected from an ad he was working on. Ogilvy said, "Make it immortal!"[3]

3. *Create and manage accountability around your vision through business reviews, high goals, and projects that fascinate.* We wrote earlier about Greg Goff at ConocoPhillips, who created accountability around his Source Document and the billion-dollar challenge that focused on developing extraordinary leaders, coming up with powerful growth strategies, and dreaming of incredible operating efficiency by asking every business unit and individual in the company to set high goals in service of these. He also put into place a business coaching cycle (review) with every business unit three times a year. The first part of the day was spent focused on the business unit goals: What's so? What's missing? The second part of the day was spent focusing on each individual's significant leadership and business challenges—all in service of the *what* they wanted to create with the Source Document.

4. *Source key initiatives with unabashed fanaticism.* The vision and goals represent the what of the grand design. The key change initiatives—major pillars and building blocks—are the how. Most Source Documents cover three areas: People Initiatives, Strategy Initiatives, and Operations Initiatives. It is up to you to make sure that these key initiatives and the methods and tools that go with them are world class, institutionalized, and systematic. Be careful that your initiative does not gain the perception of "flavor of the month." If you, for example, dream of incredibly good operations and you have brought on a Six Sigma quality initiative, you are not going to get quality by being "in favor of quality" or just a "fan of quality." You need to be fanatical! You have to measure quality, promote people on it, and reward them for it.

5. *Periodically step back and do a "What's So" to see what is missing that will make a difference.* With your team, ask the following questions: One, in the context of our vision, what have we accomplished? What is working? Not working? Two, what is missing that, if provided, will make a difference? And three, what new goals, projects, and initiatives do we want to commit to and focus on to reach our vision? When necessary, bring people back to your message of what it is all about. People will become trapped by the problems of the moment and forget why they are doing a certain project or they will become jaded when things seem unworkable in the organization. This is normal and to be expected. Your job as the leader is to bring people back to what you are trying to create together.

Chapter 12

Become a Master Politician
The Art of Politics for Non-Politicians

 SITUATION: You see an opportunity to make a difference and have jumped into action. It seems that each step you take creates a widening arc of support and opposition. You know you have to deal with the opposition, but as you see it, playing politics is beneath you. *Get over it. To reach your goals you need to master the political chessboard.*

Robert in Three Different Coaching Conversations

James Taylor III is a thirty-nine-year-old Assistant Secretary at the U.S. State Department unit dealing with the Middle East section. He has dark hair, deep-set eyes, and a prominent chin. According to Jim, "I focus on being a difference maker rather than being a politician." Yeah, right! I joked with him, saying that John F. Kennedy once said that every mother wants her son to be president, but no mother wants him to become a politician in the process. He admitted that his strong desire to make a difference sometimes put him at cross-purposes with his seniors, which had perhaps curtailed his rise to greater power and influence and, therefore, his ability to have the impact he wanted to have. "I am open to some coaching on this," he told me.

◆ ◆ ◆

Rich Rogers is in charge of Strategy and Business Optimization for Phillips, a company that was divided up by regions. His job is to make sure the company realizes synergies through a Global Center of Excellence approach in brand management, the supply chain, sales, service, and human resources. The regional and country managers resisted this idea, saying, "Our market is different and we need a local strategy." Many of the regional managers have direct ties to the chief executive, who has decided not to push them too hard and to let things develop organically. This has left Rich feeling like he is between a rock and a hard spot. He tells me, "When you win in this company, the reason is leadership. When you lose, it's politics. I want to get better at both. Can coaching make a difference?"

◆ ◆ ◆

Carole Barrett is the supply chain manager for a major retail chain. She has come up with some novel ideas for reinventing the supply chain and introduced revolutionary software to match. She has captured the minds of the executive committee with her project, but not enough of their hearts for them to be real sponsors. She also has not spent enough time enrolling and engaging the powerful product category managers who are threatened by the changes Carole is advocating, which would not only mean staff reductions but changes in people's work habits and work processes. She asks me, "I have done great on the technical side of the change management process, poor to middling on the human side. Can you help?"

 TEACHABLE POINT OF VIEW: If you want to be successful, it takes more than leading with a vision, it takes becoming a master politician.

George Washington, Thomas Jefferson, Benjamin Franklin, Abraham Lincoln, Franklin Delano Roosevelt, Mahatma Gandhi, Winston Churchill, Martin Luther King, Nelson Mandela, Lyndon Baines Johnson, and Ronald Reagan were all master politicians. People who govern in war and peace do politics. Leaders who change the game in business do politics. Scientists who win the Nobel Prize for their research do politics. Activists who lead the charge to improve community schools do politics. Even great artists who represent a new school do politics.

Sure, politics can feel like kissing up, but what feels like kissing up to one person can feel like gaining the necessary power and influence to accomplish great things to the next. In the same sense, politics can be frustrating and infuriating. But what is frustrating and infuriating to one person can feel like an exciting human puzzle to another. Finally, politics may feel like changing what you stand for according to the audience. Yet to a political master in business or government, politics is not about changing what you stand for, it is about speaking to the issues and concerns of the audience.

A "master politician" is someone who successfully gains power and influence, and who successfully accomplishes something that brings about a profound, irreversible change.

If you want to make a difference in your world, it not only takes being a good leader and manager who sets a stretch goal and comes up with a straightforward and logical plan. It takes becoming a master politician who is successful at both gaining power and influence and at accomplishing something that brings about a profound, irreversible change. Most leaders tend to see this as an either/or proposition. Either they focus on clawing their way to the top and ignore making a difference, or they focus on making a difference and ignore the need to achieve a power base that will allow them to do so. To have a real impact, you have to transform this either/or dilemma into a both/and proposition.

A story from John F. Kennedy illustrates why gaining power and influence is so important. "I wanted to have some kind of positive impact on the country. But in the House you were one of 435 members. You have to be there many, many years before you get to the hub of power and influence or have an opportunity to play any role on substantive matters. After I had been in the House for six years, I made up my mind that there was greater opportunity to function in the United States Senate. In the same way, during my years in the Senate I've come to understand that the presidency is the ultimate source of action. Take the Taft Hartley Labor Bill, for instance. In 1958, I had worked for two years on that bill. President Eisenhower made one fifteen-minute speech, which had a decisive effect on defeating it in the House—two years versus one fifteen-minute speech."[1]

> *Becoming a master politician involves mastering the nuances of the political chessboard and moving like a creative artist amongst the tangle of conflicting views and confusing forces. (James MacGregor Burns)*

In the same sense, just gaining power and influence is not enough to make you a master politician. Just consider the number of presidents of the United States, company chief executives, coaches of professional or nationally ranked college sports teams, or even chiefs of local police departments that got to the top but failed to leave a lasting legacy. The ability to make an irreversible change requires taking into account that the closer you get to the top, the greater the competition is for power and resources. Thus you need to not only embrace the political nature of all organizations but also, as noted historian James MacGregor Burns said about FDR and the New Deal, "move like a creative artist amongst the tangle of conflicting forces and confusing interests."

Becoming a Master Politician— Seven Key Guiding Principles

What does it take to be a master politician? It involves knowing who you are, what you stand for, what your goals are, and how to handle yourself in the midst of conflicting agendas and shifting power grids on the corporate (enterprise) chessboard. The fact is that trying to bring about change always creates competition, which in turn creates politics. The worst mistake you can make is to assume that you don't have to be a politician or that politics doesn't exist. Here's what you need to do:

1. *Realize that style supersedes substance.* Your manner often speaks louder than your message. Many political sages have suggested that Ronald Reagan was the most effective president of our lifetime because of his policies and programs. However, if you are like most Americans, you probably aren't even sure what his policies and programs were. What people do remember is Reagan's style. His greatest strengths were his incredible affability and boundless optimism. Reagan possessed firm convictions Americans could identify with and unerring political instincts. He took the presidency away from Carter by saying, "It is morning in America," when Carter was sounding like a prophet of doom and asking, "Are you better off today than you were four years ago?" *Your Coach (In a Book)* asks, Are you likable?

2. *Stand for something that has broad appeal and addresses real human needs and wants.* Master politicians not only have great style, they also stand for something. Nelson Mandela stood for the end of the dreaded apartheid and the liberation of blacks in South Africa, enduring twenty-five years in prison under conditions that might have made Jesus Christ bitter. His stand spoke to millions, turning the tide of popular opinion among

both whites and blacks until he was set free from Robben Island prison, and in the process freeing millions of others as well. He never took the opposition personally, even inviting his one-time jailors to his presidential inauguration. *Your Coach (In a Book)* asks, Are you taking a stand for something that meets people's real needs and wants?

A campaign is an operation or series of operations in a competitive environment energetically pursued to accomplish a purpose.

---

3. *Create a campaign that captures hearts and minds.* So you want to be chief executive, get your capital budget for your game-changing ideas, or be a difference maker for your employees, customers, and constituents? The required teachable point of view is that you will need to consciously and intentionally conduct a campaign to reach these goals and aspirations. Campaigns involve winning the hearts and minds of people. FDR engaged people in his 1936 election campaign, using the key phrase, "I join with you . . ." He was determined not just to influence public opinion but also to dominate it, proclaiming in speech after speech the New Deal as a legitimate role of government. *Your Coach (In a Book)* asks, What is in the hearts and minds of the people around you?

4. *Before you map your strategy, map the political chessboard.* To gain support for your campaign and diminish opposition, think about the different players on the political chessboard and how you need to strategically influence each individual or group. Consider these seven categories of players: *inheritors* of the status quo such as kings, chief executives, supervisors, and their attendant courtiers, *opposers* who reject the change or seek another course, *partners* who align and support, *coalition builders* of like-minded partners and opposers, *splitters* who lead factions, *passives* who support the status quo by doing nothing, and *isolates* who are alienated from the process. Figure out how you can spin what you are saying so that it speaks to people's listening. *Your Coach (In a Book)* asks, Who are the people you most need to influence? How can you speak to their listening?

5. *Do whatever it takes.* People who develop power and influence and make a difference practice management by Machiavelli. The following story makes the point: When JFK returned to Boston from his PT109 experiences in the Navy, he decided to run for Congress in the North End district, which was heavily Italian. He put together a great campaign relying on the many friends he had made in college and in the Navy. His campaign manager found out that there was someone running in the district whose name was Russo. Fearing that candidate would win the entire Italian vote because of his name, the campaign manager found another Russo and asked him to put his name on the ballot, thus splitting the Italian vote. The young JFK won the election by a large margin. The Machiavellian approach is often not spoken of, but just as often done. *Your Coach (In a Book)* asks, What you can learn from this?

6. *When your support is tenuous and the opposition strong, wheel and deal to move your agenda forward one piece at a time.* Master politicians often succeed gradually rather than dramatically. FDR, who took a stand to end the Great Depression, had great style and substance as well as an exquisite sense of political timing. In his first hundred days in office, when his support was tenuous, he engaged in transactional leadership, wheeling and dealing with leaders in Congress to come up with some important reforms, holding back for the time being on those reforms that might represent a profound and irreversible change. When your power and influence are weak, be willing to ask, "If I do that for you, what will you do for me?" *Your Coach (In a Book)* asks, What people or groups do you need to give something to to gain something from now?

7. *Build coalitions of unlikely stakeholders to increase support, diminish opposition, and drive your political and business agenda through.* FDR realized during his reelection campaign in 1936 that he would have to be more of a transformational leader and act more boldly to reach his goals and in the process redefine the Democratic Party. To accomplish this he set about building coalitions in far-flung quarters that would allow him to dramatically increase support and to diminish resistance. He brought together northern Democrats and conservative southern Democrats (now Republican types like Tom Delay, Newt Gingrich, and Strom Thurmond), labor and management, populists and old

guard liberals in a sweeping electoral victory. This enabled him to enact—in what is known as his "second hundred days"—a torrent of legislation amounting to an Economic Bill of Rights, and whose programs (like Social Security, Medicare, Unemployment Insurance) still exist today. *Your Coach (In a Book)* asks, What like-minded stakeholders (or opposers) do you need to build a coalition with?

TEMPLATE FOR ACTION

1. *Learn to be charming and disarming—someone people can do business with.* One of the virtues that the greatest leaders have is that they are charming and disarming to friend and foe alike, rather than belligerent or arrogant. They combine strong will and humility in a manner that is enrolling and engaging. Margaret Thatcher said of Gorbachev that, even though he took strong positions on issues, he was someone she could do business with. Ask five people you know to rate how likable you are on a scale of 1 to 5. Then rate yourself on how likable (charming and disarming) you are on the same scale. Notice any differences.

2. *Figure out how to gain power and influence in your enterprise by using history as a prologue.* Many people would like to make a difference, but give up early in the game because they don't know how to get power. One good way to get power is to study up on the unofficial history of your company—who got into power, how they did it, and where the bodies are buried. The unofficial history isn't always accurate, as history gets interpreted by the winners. But it will show you how politics plays out at your company—how far people will go and what happens when you lose. These are the kinds of things you will never see in an annual report.

3. *Practice "push polling" bosses, colleagues, and customers.* Don't just sample public opinion, shape it. You probably know some of the crying needs of the people in your enterprise and have some ideas about what's missing that would address these needs. Push polling involves talking about issues (such as the need to grow your business or come up with innovative products) and then putting out an idea that has the potential to make a difference as a kind of trial balloon. The idea is not just to find out what people's opinions are but also to shape them.

4. *Take a stand through a rousing speech or written manifesto.* Declare an Impossible Future that addresses followers' unmet needs and wants and thereby mobilizes their support. Include an empowering vision and values and key initiatives and programs that you want to create buy-in for, outlining where people can find a place to contribute and fulfill their own needs and wants. Once you do this, personify the vision or values you are standing for through your speaking, listening, and actions so that people begin to associate what you are standing for with you.

5. *Kick off your campaign with a thirty-second "elevator speech."* A good way to get a campaign moving is to develop a short speech you can dash off as circumstances require. For example, when the chief executive, the vice president of IT, or the shipping manager gets in the elevator with you and presses the button for the fifth floor, by the time they have gotten off, you have made your point. They know what the issues are and what in your opinion is missing that would make a difference in addressing them. It's also a good idea to have a three-minute "cafeteria speech" and a ten-minute "conference call speech."

6. *Transform power wielders into powerful allies by solving their problems.* First get exposure to leaders at the executive level rather than the operative level by taking a job in close proximity to them—as, for example, an expert in the field, a chief troubleshooter, or even an executive assistant. Then solve the leader's problems. Discover the red-hot issues of power wielders and see how to frame whatever you are proposing in a way that addresses the problems. And finally, sing from the same song sheet. Donald Rumsfeld, Secretary of Defense, has an aggressive agenda but is constantly quoting G. W. Bush in his speeches.

7. *Start building coalitions by creating a relationships map.* Take a sheet of paper and fold it in three columns. In the first column write down all your goals, intentions, and major milestones. In the second column write the names of people whose help you need to get where you are going and those who need your help to get where they are going. In the third column, write down names of people who may be opposers.

8. *Practice the law of reciprocity.* A lot of people have difficulty asking for what they want. It is great to go out and ask people for their vote at the next board meeting. Yet the law of reciprocity says that people

like to be paid back. A great campaign involves reaching out to potential allies and swapping inspiration and influence, as well as practical assistance.

9. *See opposers as human beings, not as enemies.* Shimon Peres once told me that when people oppose you there is a tendency to see them as enemies with horns on their heads. Take the time to talk with your opposers, so that you can see that they are human beings with dreams, aspirations, and fears that you can relate to. Ask people about their issues and concerns, listening whether you agree or disagree and beginning to look for common interests.

10. *Deal with hot meetings that could blow up by striking the high note.* It is our observation that everyone has common goals, even in the most conflicted situations. Both the Palestinians and Israelis want their children to be able to walk down the street in safety. Therefore it is good to begin every meeting by declaring something everyone is committed to, even if there are many conflicts as to how to get there. "We are all here because we are committed to profitable growth on a sustainable basis." Once people see they have some common interests, they are more willing to look beyond their stuck positions and cooperate and collaborate.

11. *Negotiate to get 80 percent of what you want today.* You can always come back for the other 20 percent tomorrow. Develop a sense of political timing by thinking two to three moves ahead. Bill Clinton came into office with a vision of providing health care to all Americans, which was blocked by the Republican Congress. Newt Gingrich, former Speaker of the House, said of Clinton that he had to learn that you can eat an elephant in small bites. According to Gingrich, if he had come with 30 percent of his health care bill the first year, they would have passed it. Then he could have come back the second year and got another 30 percent passed, and by the third year, he would have had everything he wanted.

12. *Publicize all wins; toot your horn.* Find a variety of ways to verbally (and visually if possible) publicize all wins and accomplishments to the powers that be, as well as to everyone who will be affected by your initiative. Generously and magnanimously acknowledge all people and groups for their contributions. Be willing to repeatedly say, "I did this . . ." or "We did this . . ."

Chapter 13

Lateral Leadership

How to Lead When You Are Not
in Charge—Build Coalitions
That Increase Support and
Diminish Opposition

SITUATION: You've discovered that leaders get things done
in three ways when they are not in charge: charisma, force
of argument or pressure, and coalition building. What is the
best way forward for you? *Here's a great mentoring tale.*

Robert in a 360-Degree Feedback Interview with a Four-Star Admiral

As you get off the Metro from Reagan National Airport and approach the Pentagon you see handsome young soldiers, sailors, and marines in dress uniforms, hair neatly cropped, all appearing to be on some kind of mission. For a civilian there is something about walking into the door of the Pentagon that makes you feel like the lead in *Mr. Smith Goes to Washington*—humbled before the great institutions of state, but nonetheless swelled up with a sense of self-importance.

Today I am here to get some 360-degree feedback from Bill Faxon, a four-star admiral, on a political appointee I am coaching, the Assistant Secretary of the U.S. Navy. I am met by a polite young lieutenant who escorts me through the long Pentagon halls—lined with pictures of "Old Ironsides" (the USS *Constitution*) embattled off the Barbary Coast, Teddy Roosevelt at San Juan Hill, and the battle scene at Iwo Jima. Every question I ask along the way is answered with a cheery and polite, "Yes, sir" or "No, sir."

When we reach the long antechamber to the admiral's office, there are other lieutenants, commanders, and captains bounding around, as well as executive assistants, military assistants, and secretaries. The admiral comes out and shakes my hand, and invites me into his huge office, filled with American flags, Navy flags, and other memorabilia from his days as a battlefield commander in Vietnam, Bosnia, and the Gulf War. He has strong, deep-set eyes that reflect the steely decisions he must have made under fire, but as he gives his feedback for my coachee, he also reveals a kind and compassionate side.

"I'll give you one about your guy, the Secretary. We have a good relationship and I think highly of him. His strength is that he is brilliant and very hard working and he really has taken a stand for the future of the U.S. Navy, especially in terms of developing new warfare capabilities. He has a strong vision and gets people to see all the possibilities by presenting out-of-the-box solutions. And he is very good at taking an acquisition like the next-generation Joint Strike Fighter and establishing a business case for why we need it."

"What do you see as his 'biggest gap'?" I asked.

He replied, "His biggest gap is a result of the time that he spent on Capitol Hill working as a staffer on the Senate Appropriations

Committee. He sometimes gets too interested in pleasing people up there. He also tends to do too many deals himself and not leverage his organization."

"What do you see as his 'winning strategy'? We say a winning strategy is the source of his success, which is now a limitation."

"The source of his success was being a one-man band, someone who got everyone dancing to his music because he aligned himself with the powers that be. That strategy has become somewhat of a limitation for him today, because he has to get people from many different competing special interest groups to buy into his programs, and he doesn't have the raw power to make this happen.

"The programs he wants to get budget approval on are getting hung up due to the different special interest groups, which include powerful Senators and Congressmen on the Hill who want defense contracts in their states, the military—who always want more warfare capability than they can get budget for—and industry, who is only interested in making a profit for shareholders."

When I asked the admiral to give me his advice as to what my client needed to do to be more effective, he provided a teachable point of view that would be useful for any executive in business or government with a powerful change agenda but without the clout to make it happen—tomorrow or the day after. This teachable point of view provides a powerful antidote to the frustrations of having many voices around you, all of which can say no to your change program, but few of which can alone say yes. Let's let Faxon articulate it for us.

 TEACHABLE POINT OF VIEW: Forget charisma and might. Build coalitions that generate support and dissolve opposition.

Lateral leadership—leading when you are not in charge—involves learning to enroll, cajole, and convince people.

"Admiral Faxon," I said, "people who want to make a difference are the initiators of change. The inheritors of the status quo are often the resistors of change. As is often the case, the people who are the inheritors are often in positions of top-down leadership bearing the title of chief executive, president, executive vice president, admiral this, admiral that, and so on."

"Yes," said Faxon. "It's one thing to lead when you are in charge of a big organization. The question is, how do you lead and actually make a difference when you are not in charge?"

I responded, "One of the best strategies I have discovered involves fundamental shifts in our thinking about leadership, for example a shift from top-down to lateral leadership."

"I like that idea," said Faxon, "but I think that both are needed. In fact, I see three ways a leader can get things done in the face of resistance. The first is to have a powerful position like being the president of the United States or a four-star admiral, together with having so much charisma and the capacity to generate so much electricity that everyone does what you want. General George S. Patton possessed this quality and demonstrated it throughout World War II. There is something to be said for that kind of power.

"The second thing you can do is to try to obliterate people that oppose you. When Saddam Hussein came into power with the Baath party, he said he was modeling his leadership on Nebuchadnezzar and Joseph Stalin. This approach can work for a while, but before long, your enemies band together and attack you.

"I like the third approach, which involves what you have called 'lateral leadership' or how to lead when you are not in charge. Lateral leadership involves realizing that you can't bring about real change in an enterprise all by yourself. Most Senate chairmen, four-star admirals, and Fortune 500 chief executives are good at commanding and twisting arms, but this is seldom enough to change the face of things. You have to learn to enroll, cajole, and convince people."

Transform individual authority to collective authority
by building coalitions of like-minded stakeholders.

Whether you are at the top of the corporate ladder, a good soldier in the middle, or a revolutionary on the fringe, you have to realize the limitations of your own power and create coalitions. In so doing, you begin to escalate your individual level of power and authority to a collective level of power and authority. It is easy to scoff at people with a revolutionary idea when they speak in an isolated or fragmented way. Yet when they present themselves as a real coalition and speak as one voice, it is hard to pretend you don't hear them. It is easier to shoot down one wild duck out of the sky than it is to shoot down a whole flock.

In Washington, the Secretary of Defense sees that, to fight a global war on terrorism, you have to transform the military, which requires among other things a much higher level of collaboration between Air Force, Army, Navy, and CIA. In keeping with that, the Secretary of the Navy (in charge of Acquisitions) now decides he wants to do something that he doesn't have the authority for—say, build a walkie-talkie that is interoperable for all the services—which sounds like a good idea, but is likely to evoke resistance as each branch likes to do its own thing. He might build a coalition by campaigning for his idea and seeking out potential allies who have something at stake in it. For example, the CNO (Chief of Naval Operations), who is very forward thinking, the Assistant Secretary in charge of Acquisition from the Army who has a limited budget for radios, a key congressman who thinks like the Secretary of Defense, and a particular defense contractor who sees this joint approach as an opportunity.

TEMPLATE FOR ACTION

1. *Learn to stop commanding and threatening and start enrolling and cajoling.* Enrolling is the art of presenting your idea in a seductive way so that people see the opportunity in it for them. It is important not only to beat your own drum but to draw people out so you can understand what motivates them and help them discover the opportunity in your idea for them. It goes something like this: Let me tell you about a difference maker of an idea. . . . As this is a new idea, it doesn't fit into any of the standard organization boxes. . . . I know you have a strong interest in making a difference and might be interested in this idea for these reasons. . . . Can I count on your support?

2. *Make a rousing speech or create a manifesto intended to infect people with your idea.* You might follow a format like this: This is how

the world is changing, from [some condition everyone likes or can live with] to [something that clearly needs to be dealt with]. . . . This is how we need to change to respond to it. . . . Here is a big idea that represents what's missing that could make a difference; and here are some key projects to act on now. Build an e-mail list of others who might share your views and contact them. Put your idea manifesto on the company Web site and create online discussion groups where people can join in. Invite people to brown bag lunches or evening salons to build out the idea while you identify potential team members. Be patient! The rate of infection with any new idea virus is slow at first and then networking effects take over and it spreads like wildfire.

3. *Pick your targets and begin building coalitions of like-minded stakeholders*. Lead laterally by recognizing the limits of your power and building coalitions that will augment it: Pick your targets, such as an individual or group of individuals that can pull the levers of power. Walk down the hall and talk to the guys in marketing, production, or human resources who might have something at stake in seeing your idea come to pass. Go visit strong potential coalition partners with something at stake in your idea even if they work in another enterprise or industry, or live thousands of miles away. Locate outside experts who can lend credibility to your cause.

4. *Find a common project or task for your coalition, as that will help it grow stronger*. A group of individuals or organizations talking about the problem is not a coalition. A coalition starts to think of itself as such through common experiences and joint actions. A coalition needs to develop specific approaches, strategies, and time lines that are action-oriented. Spread credit and praise for those who complete coalition tasks. To strengthen your coalition, brainstorm five stimulating tasks you could invite people to participate in that would make your coalition stronger. For example, come up with a straw dog version of your Idea Manifesto then circulate it to like-minded stakeholders. Place at the top of each page in red letters, DRAFT! PLEASE COMMENT.

5. *Transform your grassroots movement into a mandate by choosing your moments*. You have put a lot of energy into campaigning for your idea with your manifesto and you have now garnered enough support to reach the "tipping point." It is important to pick those moments to

ask for a mandate from the powers that be or from—as we say in the U.S. of A.—"We the people." Now is the time to go to the person in your enterprise, whether it is the chief executive or the business unit president, who can both make a decision and make it stick, and make your case for a mandate.

Here is a story to inspire you. Bill Jackson, a manager we worked with, spent two years enrolling people in his "Integrated Sourcing" program—which in a nutshell reduced suppliers, producing economies of scale and major savings. He got a lot of pushback from turf kings who said, "We don't want to do this" and "It can't be done." So he began creating a grassroots movement by asking individual groups what they could save if they took this approach. Sensing the moment was right, he marched into the chief executive's office one day, spoke for three minutes about his idea, and then presented the prize—$500 million in savings guaranteed. The chief executive signed off immediately.

Chapter 14

Take an A Player in Every Job

Coach B's, Redeploy or Release Chronic C's

 SITUATION: You are beginning to wake up to the fact that you cannot create an Impossible Future with a team of chronic C players. You'd give anything for a team of A players, if only it were possible. *Now it is!*

Michel in a Coaching Conversation with an Electronics Company Executive Vice President

"Patrick Lamonde has a Napoleonic air," a colleague told me on the plane. "Though understated, he exudes authority and can be intimidating. Watch out, Michel!" I laughed this off and then reached into the pocket of my airline seat and pulled out a copy of *BusinessWeek*. There he was on the cover, Patrick Lamonde, "Business Manager of the Year." He even looked like Napoleon, with a curling lock on his brow. And here he was executive vice president of the consumer division of Phillips Electronics, sixty years old, gray hair, dark blue suit, gold and red silk tie. I thought to myself, How am I going to make a difference with this guy?

I met Patrick at a special dining room at the Paris train station. Despite my concerns, Patrick and I created an easy familiarity by speaking in French. He told me he had a "Strategy for the Future" presentation to make to the board soon, but was not making much progress on it. "Generally, I am very good at creating strategies and designing their implementation. But, Michel, I am almost embarrassed to say that I am spending all my time working one or two levels below my own and micromanaging my fifteen direct reports on operational issues. I believe I am facing a real talent shortage and I would like to talk to you about this. This is where I think you can make the most difference."

I explained that one of the things that we emphasize with all the executives we coach is that, to deliver extraordinary results, they need to create an extraordinary leadership team. The only way to do this is to take an unequivocal stand to have an A player in every job, rather than merely putting up with or trying to change the situation. "Let's look at your team," I said. "How many A players do you have? How many B players? How many chronic C's?"

When Patrick asked for a clear definition of an A, B, and C player, I responded, "A's tend to be extraordinary leaders who consistently deliver results that are beyond and out of the ordinary. B's are good as leaders and deliver what's expected. Chronic C's may have some leadership qualities, but are full of reasons and excuses when it comes to producing results. Or they do the reverse—produce results but lack leadership. I can get more specific if you like."

"Michel, that's an intriguing way to look at it," he replied. "I guess I have too few A and B players and too many chronic C's who are never going to deliver. I need to make some tough people decisions." We came up with a people strategy of rating all the players on his team A, B, or C based on specific criteria that he believed the job required. The second part of the strategy was to keep the A's, coach the B's, and redeploy the chronic C's.

Within six months, Patrick not only came up with a new strategy for the future of his company but created a high-performance team of nine direct reports—three A players, three B's he'd decided to coach more intensively, and three new hires from outside, rated either as A's or as having A potential. As Patrick said, "We need to reinvigorate the corporate gene pool."

Some months after our coaching sessions had ended, Patrick called me back. He reported that things had really changed—he had become much more demanding of his A players and was spending more time coaching the B's. The reason for the call? He wanted help in embedding a top-grade people process throughout the organization.

 TEACHABLE POINT OF VIEW: Take a stand for having a talented A player in every leadership job within twelve months.

> *Boss work is talent work. Larry Bossidy spends 70 percent of his time on the people process.*

A few weeks after my meeting with Lamonde, I picked up a copy of the *New York Times* with a story in the sports section about George Steinbrenner, owner of the New York Yankees (alias "the boss," alias "Dr. Jeykll and Mr. Hyde") flipping his lid with his general manager, Brian Cashman, for losing star pitcher Andy Pettitte on the free agent market to the Houston Astros. Steinbrenner is known for having no qualms about firing managers and clear-cutting a team's roster in order to get more talented players. I have read similar things about the leaders of ballet and theater companies, as well as Hollywood movie producers.

Today, with relentless competition here to stay and the notion of stable lifetime employment in big companies gone forever, the same thing is beginning to happen in business. Smart chief executives take a stand for an A player in every job and mean business. Ed Michaels, who wrote an article called "Talent Wars" for McKinsey, argues for a tough talent turnaround strategy. He believes that in this way, companies can increase their market capitalization by 50 percent in three years. Steve Macadam at Georgia Pacific (forest products) changed twenty of his forty box plant managers so as to put more talented, higher-paid people in the job. The result? He increased profitability from $20 million to $40 million. Amazing!

Talk sports, talk opera, talk the arts, and the conversation will be about talent. Talk finance department and the conversation will be about bean counting.

The best chief executives make talent a 24/7 obsession. At General Electric, before CEO Jack Welch retired, people marked their calendars with the day that Welch's helicopter would fly in and would visit each division for a Talent Review with his top human resource people to personally evaluate the leadership and business results of the top thirty or so people, with a commitment to getting an A player in every job.[1]

Welch showed up in these Talent Reviews as if they were a contact sport. He'd say things like, "This guy is brilliant A player; let's give him a promotion and a healthy dose of stock options," or "This guy is a strong B player with potential; let's identify his development needs and get him a coach," or "This guy is a turkey—a chronic C; it's time to release him."

Jeff Bezos at Amazon.com recruits great people by discussing their track record of developing great people.

By contrast, most leaders delegate star searches to others and pay only lip service to talent reviews, and on top of that, are highly reluctant when making tough people decisions, even when their direct reports reverse-delegate work to them so that they wind up working on weekends. If this is the situation that you are in, it is time to take a stand for creating an A player in every key leadership role on your team. You want to follow Jack Welch's example— promote the A's, coach the B's to become A's, and redeploy (or release) the chronic C's. Give yourself a time line of twelve months to do this. You will be amazed at how much more empowered you feel with a team of A players, and how much more you will personally and collectively be able to accomplish.

Empower People by Standing in Their Greatness and Extending Them an A

Once you decide to keep people on your team, extend them an A, keeping in mind that it is impossible for people to succeed in an environment where their boss views them as a chronic C or D. In other words, start relating to people right now as if they were A players, even if they are only A's in the making. Then, standing in people's greatness, coach them to set high goals that are achievable and give them feedback in the context of being an A. For example, "Kim, I see you have the potential to be an A player and make a powerful contribution to this lab. Now I have some feedback to give you in that context about a few areas where you can make some improvements."

Take Responsibility for Coaching Leaders to Make the Quantum Leap from B to A

One of the most powerful roles of a leader is to develop other leaders. For example, one day Jack Messler, business unit general manager of a manufacturing company, was at an executive team meeting with his boss, Frank Holmes, the executive vice president. Jack was explaining the power of our one-year Action Coaching program that was helping him create A players out of B players. Holmes said, "That's great at your level, but I am not sure we have time for that at my level." "Why not?" Jack asked. "Just what do you think your job is, Frank?"

TEMPLATE FOR ACTION

1. Put talent at the top of your agenda and keep it there. Take a look at your schedule for the past three months. How much time did you put into each of these three processes: people, strategy, and operations? If you come up short on the people side, make a commitment to creating an A player in every job—and dedicate 25 percent or more of your time to doing so. This means personally being on a talent quest for great people, making sure those great people are in a quest for great projects, and personally coaching and mentoring them (not hovering over them).

2. Create a rating system for ranking people. Talk over with a coach or thinking partner your decision to create an A player in every key leadership role. Then come up with a way to rate people A, B, or C, either formally or informally.

3. Define the characteristics of an A player in your organization. For example: demonstrates leadership initiative, collaborates well across boundaries, performs beyond what's expected, and personally lives the company values.

4. Get job-specific in your rating. For example, the criteria for a vice president of a business unit might read as follows: "To be an A player: be an enthusiastic leader, be a good deal maker, exhibit strong thinking processes, and demonstrate financial acumen."

5. Once you rate the people, decide on a go-forward plan. Discuss your opinion with your coach, and get a second opinion or use 360-degree feedback interviews if possible. Be prepared to make some decisions with edge. Who will you promote? Who will you coach to be an A or a B? Who will you redeploy or release? Keep in mind that it's sometimes better to remove someone from a job where they can never be an A player than it is to keep them there and allow them to struggle, knowing inside that they can never win.

6. Develop a coaching plan for all your A's and B's. Again, the leader's job is to develop leaders at all levels of the organization. Start with having each person set a significant business challenge as well as a leadership development challenge. Either give them a coach or schedule regular coaching meetings (every two to three weeks) with you where together you look at what has happened, what is missing that will make a difference, and what's next in producing the business and leadership breakthrough goals.

7. *Set up powerful coaching relationships with each of them.* Tell every person on your team that you are extending them an A for the year and that you stand for their success with respect to their strengths and gaps. Also make it clear that you are ready to coach them in that context. It is important to keep in mind that some gaps represent behavior that is transformable and others do not. For example, you cannot coach someone to have a higher IQ or superior thinking processes, but you can coach them to be more people-oriented and be much better communicators.

Chapter 15

Stop Being a Victim of Your Calendar

Start Focusing on What Makes a Difference, Not What's Merely Important or Trivial

 SITUATION: Your increasing inability to control your agenda has left you resigned and frustrated. You are spending way too much time reacting to the day-to-day demands of managing the business. You are wondering how you will ever be able to spend more time on activities that will truly make a difference. *Here are the hidden keys.*

Michel in a Coaching Conversation with Three Leaders in a Fortune 500 Company

It is another windy, mercurial day in England. The guys flying in—Joachim Asmussen from Sweden, Neil O'Carroll from Ireland, and I—have been invited for dinner by Bob Hassler and his wife Janet to their spacious home in the English countryside. It is the evening before an all-day coaching session with Bob and his leadership team, and we are all in the mood for a good, spirited conversation.

As we step into the dining area, we are struck by the awesome beauty of the view through the large window at the back of the house. As dinner progresses, I make two observations. The first observation has to do with making time and space for creative reflection. Bob speaks with enthusiasm about the immense horizon that he looks at every morning before driving to the office, "It really has an impact on me. Since I have moved here, I've had some really creative thoughts here by this window. It seems hard in the normal course of everyday business to get the proper space for any kind of reflection. As soon as I step into the office, I feel like the walls close in on me as I spend the entire day in back-to-back meetings or responding to urgent requests."

The second thing I notice is that the view of the sky changes every ten minutes. One moment huge dark clouds are invading it, then sunshine pierces through, then it rains. I think to myself that this is a lot like most days in any business: unpredictable, capricious, with sudden changes in the environment, and all one seems to be doing is responding to those changes.

As I share my observation with my colleagues, the conversation picks up. Everyone talks about how hard it is for leaders to devote the proper amount of time to dreaming, thinking, and creating. And these are not guys playing cards in a diner. They are in a position to make a difference, to create something new, to bring their businesses to a new place. Yet, at the same time, they are stuck spending the majority of their time responding to what is directly in front of their noses.

Neil, less upbeat and energetic than usual, asked, "Michel, how do we stop being caught in the corporate Bermuda Triangle where time disappears and is never to be found? How can we spend more time on those things that are not as urgent, but are so critical for the future?"

Everyone turned to me with a look that betrayed a deep-seated hopelessness around this issue, along with a glimmer of hope that maybe, just maybe, I had the magic pill. So I had to first temper expectations: "Look, guys, this is an issue that every leader faces and it never completely goes away. What I can offer is an insightful way for choosing what you should do with your time. However, rather than look at this as a time management issue, my suggestion is that we look at it as an issue of priority."

I continued, "We always spend time on things that we consider a priority, which usually means handling the immediate business and putting out fires. The key is to step back and redefine with a fresh perspective what should be the unique priorities of someone in a leadership position—those things that if *you* don't do them, they won't get done. I can offer you a model and some tools that help you spend much more time on essential things that you are probably neglecting."

 TEACHABLE POINT OF VIEW: Manage the difference you want to make to get control of the "enemy"—your time.

Be willing to question everything on your agenda. Are these activities the best way to fulfill the legacy you are passionate about?

A leader is in a powerful and unique position to make a difference. However, only very few leaders have discovered how to spend their time in the most productive way. Most are in too many meetings and working on too many matters in which they really should not be involved. At the lower levels of management, every job has a supervisory structure with someone who makes sure that people are working on the right things. But as people go higher and higher in an organization, there is less and less supervisory structure, no one to check on how they spend their time. Sometimes leaders mistake the chaos they live in—the demands coming at them from every direction—for a useful structure for their days, but that's an illusion. In reality, what happens is that they become slaves to their calendars.

However, before you make any changes on how you spend your time, you need to understand the intrinsic accountabilities of all leaders. It is our observation that most executives have a fundamental misconception about the accountabilities of a leader, and this misconception leads to an inability to leverage their time and attention. As a leader, you need to understand the role that is unique to you. That understanding will shape what you perceive as a priority, which will lead you through your daily choices on how you spend your time. What is it that, if you don't do it, will not get done because it is part of your mandate and position? You need to step back for a moment and see with greater clarity the activities and accountabilities that belong uniquely to you and that allow you to make the difference that you want and need to make.

One key to using your time more effectively is to say no—firmly and with class. Figure 15.1 shows the four areas of accountability of leaders. If you restructure your thinking about this matter and understand where you need to focus your time and attention, you will be able to powerfully alter your behavior.

Figure 15.1. The Four Areas of Leadership Accountability.

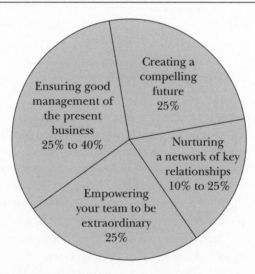

Ensuring Good Management of the Present Business

Managing the present business is the most obvious, immediate, and time-consuming role for most leaders. The opportunity here is to maximize what you've got. In our experience, the vast majority of leaders spend at least 70 percent of their time in this area. But the ideal allocation should be somewhere between 25 percent and 40 percent, depending on the circumstances. Your job as a leader should be to ensure that others provide strong management of the current organization, and then to get on with creating the vision for the next life of the organization and ways to bring the organization from here to there.

Creating a Compelling Future

The second area is simple. If you are not creating the future, no one else is doing it and it is not being done. The bottom line is that your organization will pay dearly for the lack of a compelling vision, a solid strategy, and a business model that truly supports the strategy. One CEO we coached said when we talked to him about his time, "Until today I was not focused on vision but execution. I have been concerned with the *how*—how we operated, how efficient we were. Now I see that I need to be concerned with *what*— what opportunities to pursue, what partnerships to form, what technologies to back, and what experiments to start." To do a good job, you must dedicate at least 25 percent of your time here.

Empowering Your Team to Be Extraordinary

The third area is key to creating a higher organizational capability to meet today's and tomorrow's challenges. Too many leaders are only concerned with leaving a business legacy of hard assets; they need to understand the impact of leaving a people legacy as well. People are ultimately the key to managing the business today and to implementing a new future. Your role here should be threefold: getting individuals in key leadership positions to be high performers, getting teams to be high-performance teams, and coaching the next generation of leaders. Spend at least 25 percent of your time here.

Nurturing a Network of Key Relationships

In the fourth area, your job as a leader is to create a large, power-ful, and meaningful network of key relationships. This network is crucial to the implementation of the future as well as to your pre-sent success. What is possible for your organization increases dra-matically when the depth and breadth of its relationships increase. This is true for individuals and true for organizations. As a leader, you can expand your ability to capture or participate in new busi-ness opportunities by nurturing relationship with key suppliers, key clients, key government leaders, or potential partners. Spend ap-proximately 10 percent to 25 percent of your time here, depend-ing on your situation.

TEMPLATE FOR ACTION

1. *Rigorously assess the way you spend your time.* Looking closely at your schedule can often be very shocking. We have heard, "I have to travel to the United States once a month for executive team meetings, which takes a full week," "I spend almost two days a month doing things in community activities like the United Way," "I spend more hours with taxi drivers than with anyone on my staff." Sound like you? Open your calendar, survey all your activities of the last three months, and quickly mea-sure the percentage of your time currently devoted to each of the four areas—or on matters that don't fit any of them. If you are surprised by how much time you spend in low-leverage areas, immediately make a list of the things that you are going to stop doing.

2. *Determine the ideal percentage for each area.* Assess your prior-ities and the ideal percentage to allocate to each area to fulfill your leadership role successfully. Free your mind of the current constraints. Don't settle for less. If you have ever found yourself thinking, "If I only had more time, I would . . ." think now about what you could do that would make a difference. For example, put together a Source Docu-ment containing your vision of the future, spend more time investing in relationships with potential joint venture partners in your industry, or spend more time coaching direct reports.

3. *Ask yourself about the payoff and the price of how you are spending your time now.* Identify the cost to the organization and to you of not spending the ideal amount of time on critical activities. Often the cost will be in lost opportunities. Be specific. Go to some depth. Determine what results or accomplishments would be possible in each of the four areas if you spent the ideal amount of time in each. Think not only in terms of what is possible if you increase time spent but also of what might be possible if you decrease it. For example, if you spent less time managing the present business, you might be able to expect—and get—a higher level of accountability and leadership from your team.

4. *Ask what new actions will allow you to make a greater difference.* For each of the four areas, make a list of new actions that you can commit to and that will create change immediately. Be specific about the intended results for each new action. The following suggestions may stimulate your thinking:

Running the present business: You might be working one or two levels lower than your pay grade and getting into too much detail or dealing with crises. Come up with new and less time-consuming ways to achieve certain priorities. Reduce others by delegating. Determine the key drivers for your business and create metrics for each. Create a continuous improvement program around the metrics and hold managers accountable for delivering on them. This will obviate the need for you to micromanage, while ensuring that you have a tighter ship without so many fires to put out.

Creating the future: Spend some time creating a Source Document with a compelling vision of the future, working in a team-building session or with a thinking partner. Incorporate these three areas: 1) *Social architecture.* Go out and talk to people in your organization to sense the principal mood that exists today—inspired or resigned—and then envision how you would like things to be. 2) *Strategy.* Read about and examine emerging technologies in your business that represent opportunities to be a game-changer and create the future of your industry. Look at unmet needs and wants of your customers as well your competitors' latest moves. 3) *Strong foundations.* Ask yourself and others how you can create the most efficient and effective organization to deliver on your vision.

Building a strong team: Create the vision and then go through several iterations by asking your team for their ideas for improvement. Collaborate with great minds. Design initiatives that propel the vision. Frequently revisit your vision, communicating it repeatedly to the organization. Bring the spirit of the vision to life throughout the organization. (You cannot do all this with 5 percent or 10 percent of your time.) Schedule one-on-one monthly coaching sessions with direct reports. Schedule a two-day off-site with your leadership team to align on the vision and objectives and create a line of sight to each person.

Developing a network of key people: Make a list of people and key organizations to support present success and any future you will create. The reasons for adding a name to the list may vary—for example, managing the politics, creating synergies, finding supply chain partners, or making a technological advantage. Create a road map of key relationships and prioritize them. Choose for each the best means and frequency of communication: meeting, dinner, or golf, for example. Pick up the phone and get in touch. Identify associations, conferences, fundraisers, and other groups that you should participate in. Bring key relationships together to present your vision or your new product, and to brainstorm solutions to issues and dilemmas.

5. *Commit to the deliberate implementation of your ideas.* Make the new time distribution real in your calendar. Make a no-nonsense commitment to gradually but boldly implement the changes you have identified. Don't underestimate the pull of past habits. Make a commitment to end up with a new reality for how you spend your time within three months. Be totally clear on your intention to produce extraordinary accomplishments every hour you spend. No sacred cows allowed. Schedule in your agenda your new actions and activities.

Chapter 16

Get Ready for Big Meetings Like a Championship Game

Focus on Who You Need to Be and on What You Need to Do

 SITUATION: You have a big meeting coming up that is like a championship game for your business. You want your preparation for the meeting to match the opportunity and to come home with a big win. *Learn how to get the edge.*

Michel in a Coaching Conversation with a Financial Services Executive

April 17, 2000, Amsterdam. Jan Vanderberg, president of ING Europe, walks into the lobby of the Intel hotel smoking his trademark cigar. Jan is not wearing his usual smile, however, and he grumbles when he sees me. "What's wrong?" I ask, shaking his hand.

"This coaching session is not what I need right now. It's really bad timing. I have a meeting next Monday with the board to present the business strategy and our plans going forward. This is a crucial meeting to get the support and endorsement we've got to have. And some of my colleagues are undermining our position. I am going to be hard-pressed to be ready for the board meeting even if we cancel this coaching session! I'm really in a bad mood!"

"Jan," I respond, "it is clear that this one meeting with the board has the potential to be a turning point for the future of your business. Let's scrap the agenda for today and spend our time together preparing so that you will be powerful, clear, and at the end successful with this meeting."

"I know how to prepare for meetings. What can you do?"

"A lot. When most people prepare for a meeting, they focus on what they want to say or they spend their time preparing a snazzy PowerPoint presentation. That is not enough. There is much more that you can do to really take control of the outcome of the meeting.

"For example, you need to spend time thinking about the people who will be attending and what concerns and personal agendas they will be bringing to the meeting. You need to think about whether or not you need to create more of a common understanding with them beforehand. Most important, there are things you can do to prepare yourself to be clear, powerful, and avoid reacting unproductively if surprises appear. My commitment for this coaching session is that you will be exactly 'who you need to be' for this meeting with the board, and that you will get what you want, beyond expectations . . . okay?"

A smile spread across Jan's face. "Michel, let's do it!"

For the record, we ended up extending our time together from four to six hours. Jan completed his preparation on the train back to his office and the board meeting ended up being a thunderous success. Two years later, ING Europe fulfilled on Jan's vision for the business, and looking back, Jan is convinced that the meeting with the board was a turning point.

TEACHABLE POINT OF VIEW: Big meeting on the horizon? The outcome is written in the preparation.

It's not only what you do, but what you "be."

In sports, not all games have the same importance. It is part of being a great athlete to build an inner desire to win every game, but the truth is that most games are just one more event on the calendar. And then, there are the Big Games—those defining moments that make or break the season and separate good from great accomplishments. You can say the same with business meetings. Certain meetings are like a Big Game in sports, you either come out with a win or you go home for the rest of the season defeated and depressed.

Big-Game meetings can produce a giant leap forward—or they can derail your business or create stagnation that will last for months or years. They can result in people with different views and backgrounds engaging in a dialogue that produces thrilling breakthrough solutions or they can leave you with the feeling that everyone was full of hot air—ho hum. They can leave participants feeling inspired and empowered or diminished and cynical.

First, a leader must keep an eye on the calendar and distinguish those key meetings that have the potential to be real turning points from the myriad of merely important ones.

What makes a meeting truly great is a leader who brings internationality, commitment, clarity, and flexibility.

Second, the bigger the meeting, the higher the priority you need to place on preparing deeply and thoroughly. Conventional preparation—a good agenda and a snazzy PowerPoint presentation (often put together by someone else!)—is insufficient. Our coaching is that, if you want to seize the full opportunity of the big meeting, you need to personally go to another level of ownership and prepare rigorously. The same way pro athletes prepare differently for the Big Game, you need to leave nothing to chance, you need to be ready to respond to the unexpected, and you need to be at your best.

There is no such thing as being overprepared. Churchill spent one hour of preparation for each minute he spoke. Being one of the greatest orators did not just happen by accident. Obviously in today's world you are not going to do that, but speeches, presentations, or even conversations that shape other people's thinking and actions need to be deeply and profoundly prepared.

Getting clear in your mind on the objectives you want to achieve will shape how you will think and how you will behave.

We have found that the aspects of meeting preparation discussed in the following sections are the ones most often missing.

Clarity of Intention

Clarity is power. It is essential that you become extremely clear about the purpose of the meeting and the intended results. What is the outcome? Picture it in your mind as you would like it to happen and then write it down. It is important to make sure that people know of and are aligned with your intentions, and that doesn't just happen. Inform them ahead of time or at the meeting and ask, "Are you with me in this intention?"

Clarity of Who You Need to Be in the Matter

Ask yourself, "How do I need to show up?" This point of preparation is critical—and most people ignore it completely. Think about "who will you be" in the meeting to achieve your intended results. You have the choice to draw your identity from your stand for the future and what you are committed to achieving or just going in and doing "business as usual" or winging it—which usually involves falling back on your winning strategy (habitual set of reactions) when the unexpected happens. Seeing who you are as your commitment rather than unconsciously acting from your winning strategy will tend to immediately shift your behavior. The opportunity is to stand in your commitment and call forth your highest and best self, consistent with the results you want to achieve.

Focus not just on what you need to do at the meeting, but on who you need to be.

Clarity About Participation

Think about who will participate and how you may need to shape their participation beforehand. This is a second point that is often completely ignored. To be successful, you need to know who will be at the meeting, what their issues and concerns are, and whether or not they will contribute to your intentions or oppose them. Once you have assessed people's probable participation, look at what you need to do to make sure that they are adequately prepared to participate or at what you might have to do beforehand to gain their support.

TEMPLATE FOR ACTION

1. *What are the Big-Game meetings coming up?* Look at your calendar for the next three or four months and identify your Big-Game meetings. To prepare adequately, dedicate enough time in your agenda for each of these meetings. Consider whether you should invite others to join in that preparation.

2. *Power prepare so you exceed all expectations.* That means coming up with useful answers to the following questions:

What is the purpose of the meeting? (Usually there is one overarching purpose.) For example, the purpose could be "to acknowledge and build on the progress of the past twelve months and to align on the vision, objectives, and priorities for the next two years."

What are the intended results of the meeting? List five to ten desired outcomes. For example:

To have strengthened the relationships between everyone on the team.

To have everyone on the team be ready to communicate a unified vision broadly throughout the organization so that everyone can be inspired and ready to take it on.

To have a high-quality dialogue with the group on specific operational sticking points that will lead to some innovative solutions.

What is your "ground of being" for the meeting? Write down three to five statements that express who you will be in this meeting and with people. It helps to be aware of unproductive behavior that you might fall back on under stress. For example:

I am committed to investing in people and to unleashing what is possible for each individual. (I will avoid my predictable behavior of being a hard taskmaster.)

I stand for the possibility that there is a solution when we face stuck situations or tough issues. (Rather than falling back on my tendency to avoid uncomfortable situations.)

I am passionate about our strategy and budget proposal and, at the same time, I am open to people expressing what is truly on their minds. (Rather than trying to dominate the conversation with my own point of view.)

3. *Prepare people for participation in the meeting.* Identify who needs to be at the meeting to produce the intended results. If you are not the originator of the meeting, find out who else will be attending. Take the following advance steps:

˜ Identify the strengths, commitments, and concerns of each individual coming and what they can contribute to the meeting, or any opposition they may have to your intentions.

Send people an appropriate request for preparation. Communicate to all the compelling opportunity of this meeting, the purpose and intended results, and how you expect them to participate in the meeting.

Determine if you need to talk with people before the meeting to ensure they come with the proper level of commitment and ownership.

For people who might be opposers, have a conversation with them prior to the meeting where you listen to and address their concerns, as well as help them understand (and join with) your commitments and intentions. This may involve building on common ground or trying to resolve any issues.

It is also important to try to know a little about each person who will be at the meeting (it is all about relationship!), so that you can make some kind of connection with them.

4. *Prepare what you will say and do.* Take into account the *listening* (the issues and concerns) of the participants—especially the people with the most influence and power. Think in terms of a conversation—cut down on the PowerPoint slides and avoid making a presentation that inundates people with information and puts them to sleep.

5. *Lead with power, flexibility, and intention. Be open to new possibilities.*

Create an agenda designed to accomplish the purpose and intended results and communicate this to people. But don't let yourself be stuck with the agenda. Internalize the purpose and intended results and stay centered in your intentions. Have your agenda as a structure for the conversation, but be ready to improvise and respond to what is happening or whatever direction the meeting is taking.

Lead as much with your listening as with your speaking. Listen for what people are saying and for what they are not saying. Listen generously to everyone's contribution. Pay attention to people's "background conversation" (what they are thinking but might not be saying).

End the meeting with specific actions. Who will do what, by when? Make sure that you take advantage of the new possibilities that the meeting has created and ensure that you gain the territory that is there to be taken in the next two to four weeks.

6. *Ensure that your meeting builds into action and momentum.* Following the meeting, debrief what was accomplished and what next needs to happen to build on the accomplishments. Don't let the momentum die. Think of accomplishing 80 percent at the meeting and 20 percent following it. Make sure that you and others keep promises made in the meeting. Follow up rigorously.

Part Three

Your Extraordinary Career Challenge

Do you want to become a chief executive, an executive vice president, or a general manager? Do you think you have a shot at a big promotion? Do you feel frustrated and thwarted in your present job or organization? Do you feel like you are becoming a one-dimensional cubicle dweller, even though you want an extraordinary career more consistent with your passions, talents, gifts? This section of *Your Coach (In a Book)* will show you how to find the career that's the right fit and advance your career in any organization, while at the same time supporting you in broadening out and becoming more of a complete human being. All of this is key to mastering your leadership and business challenges.

We heard a great story about Warren Buffett that gets to the heart of having a great career. Buffett was addressing a group of college students at the University of Nebraska. In his usual down-home style, Buffett said, "I am really no different from any of you," and smiled. As Buffett is one of the richest men in the world and most of the students could barely cover their cell phone bills, this comment brought a chuckle.

"I may have more money than you, but that doesn't make the difference. Sure I can buy the most luxurious handmade suit, but I put it on and it looks cheap. I would rather have a cheeseburger at Dairy Queen than a hundred-dollar meal." The students didn't quite buy it. So Buffett made a concession. "If there is any difference between you and me it is that I get up every day and have a chance to do what I love to do. If you want to learn something from me, this is the best advice I can give you. This is the secret of my success."[1]

This section of *Your Coach (In a Book)* starts by asking you to take a stand for having an extraordinary career. Ask yourself to rate your career on a scale of 1 to 10. Is it extraordinary today? If it is not, what would make it a 10? To help you answer these questions, let's take a look at three stages every extraordinary career goes through:

1. *Declaring a career path where you can shine.* You discover your talents, motivations, and interests through education and early job experiences and decide what you want to be—a CEO, a medical doctor, or an opera singer.
2. *Gaining career momentum.* You gain notice as a leader, racking up accomplishments that are getting you promoted and opening up opportunities.
3. *Reaping the rewards.* You have both great financial rewards and great recognition, as well as the possibility of spreading your wings in new directions.

How Am I Doing? Let's Do a Progress Check

To set a career goal, it is important to take a moment and reflect on how your career is going. The following questions might help:

Are you on the right career path? Do you know what you love to do with a passion—and are you doing it? Are you a CEO because you have a passion for it or because you murdered all the alternative lives you might have lived? Are you a doctor or lawyer because you love it, or because your father was a doctor or a lawyer? Are you not just competent but also masterful at what you do? Is your work play or drudgery? If you don't like the answers to these questions, it's time to have a candid talk with a coach or mentor.

Are you gaining career momentum? Let's assume you have found a career path that allows you to shine and you are sailing through your mid-career. Are you starting to show up on the corporate radar screen as a leader or high-impact player? Have you reached some high goals, initiated change, or delivered on some brag-worthy projects? Have your accomplishments been met with a number of promotions in the last few years, as well as reward and recognition? If not, you'd better get some feedback on what is in the way, keeping you from showing up as a leader who is accomplishing things.

Are you ready to reap the rewards of your career? Let's assume that you have reached the top of your enterprise, settled blissfully into middle management, or bailed out long ago and started your own successful business. You have a significant number of dollars and stock options in your piggy bank. You are loaded with talent and ability, and energized by the thought of reconnecting the dots in a different way and doing something new, different, and maybe even weird—or you may be ready to retire into the sunset.

To feel passionate about your job, get the recognition you want, and be able to reap the rewards, you need to meet the three challenges listed in Figure Part 3.1.

Career Challenge One: Finding the Right Fit: Talent, Passion, Culture

Declare a career path that allows you to shine. If you are on the wrong path, find a new one. It's later than you think.

Creating an extraordinary career depends on meeting your first career challenge, *fit*. Finding fit involves three factors. First, discovering your talents and gifts. Second, discovering your passions—the kind of roll-up-your-sleeves work that gets your juices flowing. And third, finding a company with the kind of people and culture that feel natural to you. This is a different thinking process from just finding the next step up the ladder. (See Figure Part 3.2.)

Many people in leadership positions find themselves succeeding in careers that they are not passionate about and have no value for. If you are successful at the wrong thing, then the mix of promotion, money, and praise can result in your getting trapped in the wrong place forever.

Figure Part 3.1. Three Career Challenges for an Extraordinary Career.

Career Challenge 1. Make sure that your career is a fit.

Career Challenge 2. Get to the top of your field.

Career Challenge 3. Broaden your horizons.

Figure Part 3.2. Make Sure Your Career Is a Fit.

Discover:	Strengths and talents	Passion—what gets your juices flowing	People you want to work with

For example, we knew one rapidly emerging leader in the biotech industry whose career had followed the advancement track familiar to many highly talented people, from team leader to manager to vice president.

> *Discovering your talents, passions, and cultural fit may be more important than finding the next step up the ladder.*

However, in the middle of this rapid ascent, he realized that he was in the middle of a career where success was more dangerous than failure. "I was a biology major in college and earned a doctorate. After graduation, I went into a biotech company rather than academia, because I thought that was where all the money was. However, now I see that my progress toward the top is just carrying me away from what I really want to do."

When we asked him where he thought his passions were, he said, "As seductive as the power, prestige, and money is in this company, I believe my passion is in coaching and teaching in a university." He left the company, got a job teaching in a small college, and then became a full professor at a major university. He also became an assistant coach on the school's crew team. Discovering the right fit is not something that you do at the beginning of your career and then forget about, it is an ongoing process that requires continuing vigilance.

> *It is important to see the big strategic picture of your career rather than get stuck in career myopia.*

It's a wise idea to allow your talents, passions, and gifts to pull your career in the right direction. This sometimes requires turning down what might look like a great promotion, or allowing your career to migrate from one area of a business or industry to another. All too often leaders have career myopia, which causes them to continue to fight their way up the ladder even if means giving up their real dreams or putting aside their passions.

Phil Jefferson was a business unit general manager of a big electronics firm. His vision was to become a vice president and corporate officer, which would allow him to have the status he always wanted and pull down big stock options. His company went through a merger, and the new company had no job with profit-and-loss responsibility to offer him. It offered promotion to vice president and corporate officer in a staff job, or a severance package that would give him time to look for something else.

That was a tough choice. Suffering from career myopia, Phil reached out for the promotion like a drowning man grasping a sword blade for help. Six months later, bored to death in his mind-numbing staff job, he realized he had made a terrible mistake. He then decided to leave the company and look for another general manager job that he could be passionate about, but without the package he would have gotten had he left earlier.

You may well be asking yourself some questions right now that go like this: "I have a big job in a big company, and in all honesty, what I am doing now is not my passion. So now what do I do?" Or "You've got the diagnosis right; now what's the cure?" Our suggestion is to continue in your present situation for the time being, spending 80 percent of your time on your day job, and then figure out how to spend 15–20 percent of your time on the thing that you are passionate about. This may help you bring new passion to your current job, or it may lead you to venture out and do something else entirely.

Career Challenge Two: Get to the Top of Your Field Through a Track Record of Accomplishment

Developing career momentum is a matter of both showing up as a leader and accomplishing what it is you need to accomplish.

Getting to the top of your field might mean several different things, but it usually depends on accomplishments. It could mean rising up the corporate ladder and becoming chief executive or vice president because you showed up as a leader and opened some new market space. It could mean publishing a paper on economics and winning a Nobel Prize. It could mean doing scientific, medical, or genome research and being recognized by your peers for making a contribution to the discipline that means most to you.

Getting to the top of your field requires that you have the kind of character, personality, and temperament that is passionate to the nth degree, inspiring to others, creative and effective in thought and action, able to thrive under pressure, full of curiosity and desire for learning, prepared to accomplish things when others would have given up, and ambitious as hell. Without ambition, you won't go very high or get very far, and can't expect very much.

People in big companies often genuflect before authority and suppress their ambition so as to be seen as good soldiers who get the job done. The idea is that all this self-sacrificing effort will be met with gratitude and you will receive a promotion or a raise in pay. This strategy can sometimes succeed, but just as often it will fail, especially if your boss plays the political chessboard and tends to take the credit for what you do.

Getting to the top of the ladder or at least the next rung requires becoming a virtuoso in what we have come to call the "Master Game," which involves not only having a constant grasp of your job but also a grasp of the political, economic, and human forces at play in any large organization. The ability to become such a virtuoso performer requires keeping your eye on three different priorities at the same time, even though they may seem to contradict one another, as shown in Figure Part 3.3.

Politics

Learn to love the politics of your enterprise to realize your ambitions. As you move to the top of an organization and face increasing competition for promotion and resources, it is important to master the enterprise chessboard, not just performance. This largely involves creating powerful partnerships with people at all levels of the organization, consciously and intentionally sourcing a powerful relationship with your boss, and taking a stand to make a difference and build coalitions that increase support and diminish opposition.

**Figure Part 3.3. Three Basic Strategies
for Getting to the Top of Your Field.**

Finding a coach, mentor, or career advocate

Loving the politics of your enterprise

Focus On

Racking up a track record of accomplishment

Accomplishment

Rack up a track record of accomplishment. People who distinguish themselves in any field are those who focus on making a difference, not just making a living. This involves paying attention to the customer's needs and coming up with a "wow" project that is based on what's missing. It then involves executing like mad in delivering on it. At the same time, being a difference maker is a two-edged sword. Swing it one way and you change the world and get recognized for it. Swing it another way and you are branded as a rebel, heretic, and troublemaker.

Coaching

Focus on finding a coach, mentor, or career advocate. In the normal course of events, most people have the will to advance their careers, but not the humility to ask for help in the process. (This is a mistake, because people like to help.) If your boss is not your best ally, consciously and intentionally seek out a coach, mentor, or career advocate to help you analyze your career situation, give you feedback, and offer meaningful advice. It is also important to cultivate a network of people that can give you a powerful assist in reaching your career goals.

Career Challenge Three: Broadening Your Horizons May Lead to Extraordinary Opportunities

Reaping the rewards often comes when you reconfigure your talents and abilities as a result of a learning journey.

Jon Mars was a leader in the electronics industry and was rapidly climbing the corporate ladder when we worked with him. However, Jon was feeling more and more dissatisfied with his job, so when he was offered a promotion, he wasn't sure if he should take it or pursue his passions, which by the way he was not entirely clear about. I told Jon, "You do have choices" and suggested that he write a résumé that we could use as a starting point in planning his next steps.

Jon sat down to work on his résumé. I asked him to focus not on his future potential but on his past experience, skills, and accomplishments. The exercise turned out to be somewhat of a shocker, as well as a rude awakening for Jon. "I saw in writing the résumé how narrow my life and career had been. I got my BA in business in college, then went on to the graduate MBA program. After school, I did a series of jobs following the familiar advancement track from individual performer, to manager, to business unit leader. I have spent my whole career inside this one company and not experienced very much of life. On top of that, I think I have suppressed my real passions." I talked to Jon about the importance of broadening his horizons, which sent him on a long odyssey of soul-searching and self-discovery, which eventually resulted in an exciting career change.

Jon typifies many leaders in Fortune 500 companies who think their company is the whole universe and that there is no universe beyond it. They spend their whole lives inside the same enterprise and cannot think, talk, or act outside it. Often these managers will come to us and complain, saying they want to do something else that allows them to operate in the domain of creativity and risk. Yet in most cases, when decision time comes around, they stay in the comfort and security of their refuge.

I often advise people to broaden their horizons by perhaps taking a sabbatical where they can go on a learning journey that takes them way beyond their expertise. I also suggest taking on a foreign assignment, where they won't have to breathe the stale air of orthodoxy that usually circulates around corporate headquarters—or at least taking a job in another department. These experiences can lead to new ways to connect the dots of your talent and abilities and result in new jobs or entirely new careers—like starting your own business or working for a nonprofit that is hell-bent on changing the world.

The interesting thing is that according to *BusinessWeek,* managers in Fortune 500 companies form no more than 10 percent of the U.S. workforce. It turns out that a growing number of people who used to work in big companies are now migrating to what author Dan Pink calls "Free Agent Nation."[2] Did you know that? Stable employment in Global 1000 corporations is gone. The average career will involve two to three different occupations and most people will spend at least several years self-employed. Instead of seeing this as a threat, see it as an opportunity.

One of the best ways of broadening your horizons is to establish what Tom Peters calls the "Brand Called You" and begin to see your job not as a long slog of another ten years as a cubicle dweller in a white-collar tower but as a series of gigs and "wow" projects conducted by your own professional service firm, the one with your name on it. Instead of sitting down and writing a résumé, why not sit down and write your "Unique Marketing Proposition"—which tells what you do that is uniquely you. It could be "chief engineer for hire," "retired doctor without borders," or "the world leader in executive coaching."

Do you have your career goals and priorities in order? Name one promotion you would love. Name another you should turn down.

Formulating Your Career Challenge

When taking a stand for an extraordinary career, talk through the following questions with a thinking partner.

1. *Do you have your career priorities in the right order or do you need to make a basic shift?* Are you climbing a ladder resting against the wrong building or is your career based on your real talents, passions, and strengths?
2. *What kind of job or company would be a great fit for your talents, passions, and people preferences?* Also ask yourself what kind of

company culture would constitute the right fit? It may be useful here to gather some 360-degree feedback, as well as talk to a coach, thinking partner, or person that knows you well.

3. *What do you need to do to get to the top?* What is missing that would produce a breakthrough in getting to the top of your company or profession: mastering the chessboard, making a difference, getting the job done?

4. *What do you need to do to broaden your horizons?* Where do you want to be in your career in three years? Who are the most connected people in your field, or the one you want to go into? How can you establish a relationship with them? Now, just do it!

The Chapters in This Section

Now you are ready to turn to the specific chapters in this section for some more nuggets that you can use toward creating an extraordinary career. You will learn that one of the keys to success is to have a burning ambition for power and influence, as well as for making a difference. You will learn how to network to that ambition by investing in relationships with connected people. You will also learn how to "manage up" to get ahead, as well as how to stop being a victim of your boss.

You will see that your chance of being a hot, sought-after talent is much higher if you pursue mastery, not just competence. You will also learn how to deal with derailers, a negative conversation that has developed about you that could endanger your career, and the ever-oppressive risk of burnout. Finally, you will learn how to create a powerful résumé that is an effective advertisement that gets you an interview that helps you realize your potential, rather than a postmortem of your past experiences that puts its readers to sleep.

Chapter 17

Do You Have a Burning Ambition?

Seize the Crown, Stop Being Just a Good Soldier in the Long March of History

SITUATION: You see others are getting ahead faster than you and can't figure out why. Perhaps their secret is not that they have more talent but that they have more ambition. *Your masterful coach will enable you to set your ambition free.*

Robert in a Coaching Conversation with an Executive from a Fortune 500 Company

It's six o'clock on a Friday evening in June; I'm at a New York hot spot called Jump and the place is abuzz. People have poured out of their Manhattan office buildings for drinks and snacks. Bill Elliot sits across the table from me and expresses some of his concerns about his career as mellow jazz music plays in the background. I have been told that Bill, who is a vice president, has the potential to become chief executive of the company.

Bill tells me, "Here is the good news. I have a great job in a Fortune 500 company that's built to last. I have worked smart over the last ten years, made a difference, and been promoted." He shrugs and continues, "But here is the bad news. The closer I get to the top, the more I discover lots of other people jockeying for the same position. I am not sure whether to pursue my ambition to get to the top of the ladder or to focus on making a difference or do something else. It seems like being ambitious in my company is almost seen as a character flaw, and the best way to be ambitious is to not look ambitious."

"Bill," say I, "being ambitious needs a better reputation. Let's make one thing clear. Ambition is a sword that cuts two ways and it has to be kept in balance. On one hand, it's about fulfilling the drive to get to the top. Many of the world's greatest leaders have been very ambitious. On the other hand, ambition is much more than the drive for the accumulation of wealth and power. It is about the desire to make a difference in the world. People who are great leaders have a burning ambition and do not apologize for it in any way."

We pause as the waiter sets down a couple of beers. Elliot takes a swig and asks me for an example, and I tell one from another executive coach about a friend of his named Tom who had recently been promoted to executive vice president. The coach visited Tom one day on the fiftieth floor of a Manhattan skyscraper, a floor where the walls were covered with original paintings, the rooms filled with antique furnishings, and the floors covered with lush gold carpets. The coach said, "Congratulations, you have finally made it." Tom then silently ushered the coach out into the center of the executive suite. He said, "Do you see that office way down the long hall? That's where the CEO sits. I haven't made it until I am in that office."

Tom eventually did get the job, and the coach asked him, "How did you pull it off?" He responded, "By having a burning ambition to be CEO and to have an impact. I would often look down the long hallway to the CEO's office at the other end, and one day I had an epiphany that this was to be my place. It was like I was looking down a long corridor without any doorways or fire escapes. Once I was clear about my burning ambition, I then began to ask myself who I needed to be and what I needed to do to attain it."

He continued, "I realized that I needed to show up as a leader who had an impact. I also realized that I needed to manage up to the chairman and other bosses, and that I was never going to be just be a good soldier who went into combat, lost an arm, and hoped to get a medal. One day my boss said to me, 'I need you to do this thing.' I replied, 'If I do this for you, what will you do for me?' I also made sure I touched issues and opportunities that would make a difference and I performed like hell to get the job done, coming up with creative solutions, building coalitions, and executing. Excellence stands out like a ton of diamonds."

"That's fascinating," Bill murmurs, gazing blankly at the ceiling. "Maybe I don't have too much ambition. Maybe I don't even have enough . . ."

TEACHABLE POINT OF VIEW: Develop a burning ambition to make it to the top and to make a difference.

Great accomplishments require great ambitions.

Great leaders have a burning ambition that extends beyond the accumulation of wealth and power to the need to fulfill a purpose larger than themselves. At the same time, they may pursue wealth and power as a means to an end. A burning ambition is the basis of playing a big game in life. It is the inner drive that prompts us to take charge of our own destiny rather than put it in the hands of others. Ambition is life's appetite and one of the conditions of being a healthy human being is to have hearty appetite, not just for wealth and power, but for making a difference, along with food, money, sex, and so on. In many cases, people's appetite is not too big but rather too small.

Think about how much ambition FDR had in order to become president and put an end to the Great Depression. Think of how much ambition Jonas Salk must have had to eliminate the childhood disease polio. Think about how much ambition someone like Jack Welch must have had to become CEO of General Electric and make it the most competitive enterprise on earth. Think about how much ambition someone like Jeff Bezos must have had to leave his cushy job in New York, get in his car, and go west to Seattle where he would start Amazon.com with a dream of transforming the retail industry through the Web.

Very few people are so ambitious that they have a specific image of what they want to achieve. They think about the next rung on the ladder, the next increment of money.

Giving yourself permission to *be* ambitious and take it to the top is a vital launch pad for a successful career. Yet constructing it may involve first dismantling some limiting beliefs and assumptions, like "be a good soldier and you will get ahead." Though there is always merit in being a good soldier who gets the job done in a self-sacrificing way, there is no correlation between being a good soldier and getting ahead, especially when you get close to the top and run into an increasing number of people jockeying for the same position.

The next point to get is that *clarity is power.* The clearer you are about your burning ambition, the more powerful you will be in achieving it. If you don't know what it is, dare to dream. Dream beyond the wildest possible pushing of your imagination and beyond that. Wayne Huizienga had a dream to become CEO of a big organization that combined local trash collection companies. It took less than a decade for Waste Management to go from a million-dollar business to a billion-dollar business and the largest trash collection company in the United States.

Finally, with ambition, we cast our line to the stars, standing in the future we want to create and taking action in the present to realize it. Several years ago, a colleague coached a man who came to have a very clear picture of what he wanted in his life. He wanted to own a professional sports team. Once that became clear, he worked out, step by step, what it would take to reach that goal. "To own a sports team, I have to amass great wealth. To do that, I have to be an entrepreneur. To do that, I have to learn about running a business, and that business needs to be in an industry where there's a great deal of upside potential." As he worked out the logic, it not only made a lot of sense, it also helped guide his decisions.

TEMPLATE FOR ACTION

1. *Get a thinking partner and identify limiting beliefs that cause you to play small.* We have spent a good deal of our coaching careers helping people distinguish who they magnificently are and what they are magnificently capable of from limiting beliefs and assumptions they have either inherited from society or made up. For example, in coaching leaders from Montreal (where the English culture historically dominated the French people) to "dare to dream," we often heard comments like, "My grandmother told me I was born to eat a small loaf of bread." As a result, these leaders tended to suppress their ambitions and to hold back in group meetings. The corporate equivalent of this is, "I am not going to think of getting ahead. I am just going to keep my head down and do my job like a good soldier."

2. *Declare your burning ambition and acknowledge that you're playing a big game.* You either give yourself permission to discover and express your secret ambitions—to be a CEO, an elected official, a concert pianist, and so on—or you spend the rest of your life hiding under a rock waiting for life to turn out. Distinguish between a burning ambition that you could be truly passionate about and things you are merely good at or are educated in. One woman I coached told me she had worked hard to get an MBA, but really wanted to take up landscape architecture. The next day she came back and said, "I finally decided that just because I spent $100,000 on a hammer, I don't have to spend the rest of my life driving nails." Sit down with your thinking partner and declare your burning ambition in terms of the position you would like to have as well as the impact you want to make. Write the following declaration to describe this. *I am committed to the possibility of . . . I am committed to giving up . . . to get it.* Fill in the first space with what you intend to do, and the second with the limiting beliefs you will set aside in the process.

3. *Cast yourself out into the desired future, then act from the present to make it a reality.* In coaching conversations after the exchange that opens this chapter, Bill Elliot started to become clear that he actually had a burning ambition to go beyond the business world into politics— to be a U.S. Cabinet secretary. He then began to very actively create the necessary structure for fulfillment he would need to make his ambition come true. He figured he would need to build political capital through public speaking in Washington and other places, as well as by participating in a campaign. He also figured he would need to network with people in the right places, realizing that power comes not just from your position but from the connections you make.

Chapter 18

Network to Match Your Ambition

Power Comes Not from Your Position but from How Connected You Are

SITUATION: You've got an idea of the dream job you would like to have two to five years from now. It is time to start thinking of networking as a strategic action you take toward your intended career goals and objectives. *Can we offer to be your mentor on this?*

Michel in a Coaching Conversation
with a High-Tech R&D Manager

I am sitting in a charming French café, sipping latte and awaiting the arrival of my client, Sam Bronson. Sam is manager of research and development for a very large technology company based in New Jersey. He is intelligent and hardworking and good with his people, and he produces consistent results. He is very much a straight-up kind of guy, hates corporate politics, and just wants to be left alone to get the job done. But changes are afoot in the pharmaceutical industry. Two days earlier, his company announced a merger, mentioning a major commitment to reduce staff and operating costs.

Sam is visibly downcast and worried when we meet. He tells me, "You know, Michel, for all the public talk about this being a merger of equals, from our point of view it is really closer to a takeover. Most of the new senior management, including the new CEO, are from the other company, and the buzz is that even the people in the top jobs are in jeopardy. For the last twenty years, I have had my head down. I kept driving priorities and never thought I might be in a position of losing my job. I just don't know what to do. I even found myself looking at the classifieds this morning."

"Sam," I reply, "you're a great guy with a solid track record, but listen, events like this make everyone feel a bit shaky. I am sure you have a lot of resources at your disposal, both inside and outside the company, to create your next job without resorting to the classifieds. You have been a core producer for twenty years. Let's take a look at things from the point of view that you are the center of a large network of people who know you, like you, and have a great appreciation of what you can accomplish."

While I speak, I can see Sam starting to shake his head. "Michel, you don't understand. I'm just not that kind of person. My company is my whole universe. I don't know many people, and meeting new people makes me uncomfortable. I just like to focus on the job. I've never really taken to those guys who are always bragging about how great they are. It's just more politics, and has nothing to do with producing results. I hate those games!"

"Sam, I can appreciate how certain self-promoters can be a turn-off, but that is not what I am talking about here. My job as your coach is to give you a different way of looking at the situation and a new place to stand so you can take effective action on the path to your future. To do this, you will need to shift how you view the relationships you currently have and the task of building new ones appropriate to the career you want."

Sam looks even more downcast. "Michel, I'm out of my league."

"That's okay!" I grin. "Learning new skills always makes us feel like that!"

◆ ◆ ◆

A few days later, I had a coaching session with Josh Friedman, a manager in the same company as Sam, and was struck by the difference in his interpretation of the same event. Josh held a parallel position to Sam's, and had worked for a similar period. Josh was an engaging, agreeable fellow and, like Sam, he had a track record of producing results. The one distinction between the two was that Josh had a passion for people, and during his twenty years with the company had met and come to know individuals at all levels and in all areas of the company.

On hearing the news of the merger, he saw only the opportunities it presented. He had already spoken with his boss and his peers to gauge their views, and had set up a meeting with his counterpart in the other organization. His boss had informed Josh that he was a committed advocate for him in the new organization and that, because Josh was so widely known and respected, many different roles were possible for him. In addition, Josh had received two calls from individuals outside the company who were interested in acquiring his services.

Because Josh had a clear vision of where he was headed in his career and the individuals and conversations that would assist him in achieving his goals, he did not feel threatened by the merger. He was able to remain focused on delivering his current priorities, calming the fears of those around him, and keeping his people motivated, while at the same time, being proactive in creating their future careers—all of which enhanced Josh's already strong prospects for the future.

TEACHABLE POINT OF VIEW: Think about your highest career aspirations, and then network with the intention to realize them.

Power today comes not from your position but from how connected you are.

We live in a highly individualized culture, and therefore, even in a large corporation, we have a strong tendency to see ourselves as separate entities, struggling toward our individual objectives. There may be some who are naturally gifted with "people skills" and who know lots of people, but that generally doesn't apply to many of us. We may be uncomfortable in meeting new people and, consequently, avoid doing so unless it is absolutely necessary. At any rate, we often tell ourselves that making an effort to get out and meet people is not something that we need to do to accomplish what we desire.

In reality, however, this is a highly distorted view of how human beings and human systems function—particularly in today's very interconnected work environments. We are social creatures by nature, and power depends on circulation and social interaction. In fact, in every area of human accomplishment, all achievement ultimately rests on the strength, depth, and extent of the network of relationships among and beyond the key individuals involved. To state the obvious, your ability as a manager to deliver on your objectives today is directly proportional to the relationships you have created with a host of individuals—from your current and previous bosses to your direct reports and your suppliers and your customers.

Whether we are speaking of gubernatorial candidates, talented engineers, or aspiring composers, success has always depended on their possession of a vision of themselves or of their projects far greater than the present, and on their ability to enroll others in key and prominent positions to their cause. It also has to do with the power and influence they wield through the network of relationships they have developed.

*Find out who are the people who are hubs in the network
and then find others who are linked to them.*

In an interesting article in *Fast Company,* "Desperately Seeking Vernon," Harriet Rubin writes that networking plays a role in both climbing the corporate ladder and breaking into new territory and establishing a foothold.[1] Power in today's world isn't about position. Power today means being connected in a vast spiderless web. The most powerful individual is the one with the most links to others. The article is based on work by physicist Albert-Laszlo Barabasi, who wrote a book called *Linked: The New Science of Networks.*[2]

Barabasi writes that it is a sparse network of a few powerful directors who control all the major appointments in Fortune 1000 companies. Barabasi maps the territory of corporate America by showing that the chief executives are not the stars; people in the shadows have the real control. The approximately 10,000 directorships in corporate America are held by 7,682 directors. However, 14 percent of all directors serve on two boards, and 7 percent on three or more boards. These overlapping directors constitute a close worldwide network where each is 3.5 handshakes or degrees of separation away.

*The person whose support you need may not be more
than 3.5 handshakes away.*

These are people like Washington lawyer Vernon Jordan and his wife Ann, who in 1998 sat on seventeen boards combined. Jordan currently sits on ten boards, including American Express, Dow Jones, Revlon, and Xerox. George Bush became president in part by building up a network of political allies throughout the country, primarily by sending thousands of Christmas cards. In the sports world, superagents play a key role in connecting talent and teams. These people are the hubs in the great web of relationships that links us all. Hubs are individuals of extraordinary reach, influence, and connection. If you want to increase your power and effectiveness, you need to get connected to the hubs.

What we are talking about here is *strategic* networking. It is relationship building by design. It is the deliberate and strategic action of evaluating your long-term vision and career goals in the context of the important relationships needed for success. It consists of identifying the specific individuals or networks that, because of power, reach, access, or influence, are critical to your future (the *hubs*), and then investing the time, research, thought, and creativity required to establish and maintain long-term *connections* with them.

Finally, strategic networking is the purposeful and thoughtful process by which one builds and creates a web of relationship that is broad enough, deep enough, and powerful enough to fulfill a vision or a career goal for the future. Strategic networking involves creating and standing for a long-term vision or career goal, identifying the individuals or networks of people that are important to or part of achieving that vision, and *intentionally and attentively* creating those relationships.

TEMPLATE FOR ACTION

1. *Create your future and stand for it.* Where do you want to be in your career in three, five, or ten years? What do you want to contribute to your company, your community, the world? Think big. Give voice to your deepest longings. What is your vision of where you will be in your career, or where your career will take you? Write it down. Then take a stand for this possibility. See yourself as fulfilling this vision.

2. *Identify your existing network.* Write down the people in your current network and identify, if you can, whether or not they are positioned as the hub of a powerful network of others. Is the quality, reach, and power of your current network of relationships sufficient for the future you are standing for?

3. *Identify your strengths and weaknesses as a relationship builder.* Within the context of your current network, identify habits, ways of being, or actions that have been successful for you—and those that have not. What do you feel are areas of weakness? What is missing in your ability to establish deep and lasting relationships? Make a list of all the internal reasons or blocks that stop you from taking effective action. For example, "I am uncomfortable meeting new people," "I don't know what to say or who to call." Once you have made your list, commit to putting these internal blocks to one side—and keep focused on action.

4. *Commit to building a network equal to your vision of yourself, and to mastering the skills needed to do so.* Networking is about creating and investing in relationships with people—getting to know people, making a genuine connection on a human level, and staying in touch. If you feel you lack the skills of relationship building, remember that, like any other art or skill, it requires practice and reflection. In fact, like learning a foreign language, it involves constant practice. The more you are in contact with others, the more at ease you will become.

5. *Create a project to build your network of relationships intention-ally and strategically.* Identify the key people who can influence or contribute to the future you are committed to creating. Design a long-term strategy for developing your relationship with each person. What are their interests? What are the present opportunities for meeting with each? What parts of your long-term vision is it appropriate to discuss? What questions could you ask that would generate interest in you and your future? Prepare for each conversation, and practice until you feel at ease. Be open and flexible in the actual conversation.

6. *Find a role model.* Find someone who embodies the skills, prac-tices, and behaviors that you wish to acquire, someone from whom you feel inspired to learn. Observe your model in action. Find occa-sions to talk. Ask for advice.

7. *Give yourself a break!* Have some space to be nervous or clumsy. Remember, nobody masters a new skill overnight. Most of all be open, authentic, and engaged, and maintain a commitment to the person in front of you.

8. *Be your own best manager.* Establish priorities, objectives, and time lines for your relationship-building project. Set time aside, de-brief your meetings, and follow up promptly on requests and oppor-tunities. Look for innovative ways to fulfill your project goals. Review your overall project from time to time to make the necessary adjust-ments to fulfill your long-term vision.

Chapter 19

Sourcing a Powerful Relationship with Your Boss

The Art of Managing Up to Get Ahead

 SITUATION: At best, you have good chemistry with your boss. At worst, you suffer feelings of being dominated. In both cases, you give your power away to your boss. Can you change that and have a better career? *Our answer is yes.*

Michel in a Coaching Conversation with a Financial Services Executive

Everything about Bob Thompson exudes power and confidence. His physical presence strikes you first: six-foot-three, broad shoulders, fierce and piercing blue eyes, thick blond hair turning slightly gray, and a loose and comfortable manner. In my mind, Bob is the quintessential all-American guy. I picture him in high school being the star quarterback, having more friends than a Powerball winner, and being extremely popular with the girls. And now of course, as destiny played its hand, Bob is an executive at a financial services company. Robert warned me just before my first meeting with Bob, "Michel, don't say anything to make him mad or he'll get you in a headlock. And if he does, you are dead! He has the strength of a bear."

Likewise, Bob is an impressive leader. He speaks with conviction, has an uncanny ability to recognize opportunities to create new value for his business, and can take on the toughest assignments, turning duds into assets for the corporation. The last epithet you would apply to Bob would be "powerless" or "victim." But on a beautiful and sunny day in New York City, I had the guts to do just that. (Bob spared me the headlock!)

It was midmorning and the streets were bustling with relentless activity. Bob showed up in his metallic blue Corvette, a gift to himself on his fiftieth birthday. I climbed into the car and we rode over to Central Park for a walk. "Bob, tell me what's on your mind when you try to relax? What is bugging you? What issues make you restless?"

"No business issues—I feel on top of those, but one thing that keeps getting under my skin is my interaction with my boss. I am at a loss with the guy. The truth is that he drives me crazy." His boss, Vernon Shaw, senior vice president for Marketing, is highly respected in the industry and known for his charm and wit.

He continued, "Shaw is like Dr. Jekyll and Mr. Hyde. One day, he is full of charm, inquisitive, and quite insightful in his comments and suggestions about my business. But the next day, he can be dominating, bossy, obnoxious, and downright mean. He won't ask questions; he makes assumptions and is very negative in his comments. I often leave my conversations with him feeling demotivated." Bob went on and on, providing multiple examples to support his claim that Vernon Shaw deserved the "worst boss of the year" award.

I pondered Bob's litany of complaints and finally interjected, "Bob, I hear you, and as Clinton would say, I feel your pain." (Humor works well with Bob.) "But here's the deal, how you show up to me in your relationship with Shaw is totally powerless. You speak like a victim. In all other areas of your business life and even your personal life, you always come across as someone who has the power to change the face of things. You are accountable, not waiting for the right circumstances but ready to shape circumstances to your will and intention. But with your boss, you complain like someone who has absolutely no opportunity and responsibility to create what you want.

"Bob, do you know that most people feel like you in regard to their boss? Look into your past, I bet that fundamentally you felt that same way with all your bosses. I am sure that you have had easier bosses. Shaw is a piece of work, I'll give you that. But the issue is not so much Shaw but how you relate to Shaw. Your basic premise in that relationship is one where 'the boss is in charge' and, therefore, 'he is in charge of his relationship with you.' He calls for meetings, he gives you a hard time, he acknowledges you, he presses on you, he gives you room . . . no matter what, it's all in his hands.

"Basically, you are a passive participant in that relationship, like someone who sits in the back of the bus and goes along for the ride. You suffer the relationship and hope for a boss who makes it easier for you. Sometime in your career you may have had a boss who fit well your model of the perfect boss: giving you lots of room to operate, no hands-on meddling, few meetings, and little bureaucracy. But you know, you were probably still a victim in that relationship, you were just a happy victim. You did nothing to shape that relationship. You were a slave with the right master . . . but still a slave.

"Did you ever, even with the best boss, ask yourself, 'How can I bring this relationship from okay to great? How can I create a truly extraordinary relationship with my boss that will result in extraordinary accomplishments for me, for the business, and for my boss?'"

Bob was listening with a perplexed look on his face, "What can I do to change that? The guy is still puzzling to me and the truth is that I *am* a victim in this case!"

"Here's what I can offer. You can shift your relationship with him, and with any boss you will ever have, from being a victim to being accountable, from powerless to powerful, from reactive to generative. If you want, I can show you how to do that."

"I'm ready. But I will tell you, I'm still skeptical."

Of course Bob was skeptical. There are very few role models of individuals who take full accountability to be the source of their relationship with their boss. And let's make no mistake; doing that can be a real challenge.

TEACHABLE POINT OF VIEW: Take ownership of your relationship with your boss. Shift your mindset from being a powerless victim to being the author.

Do you show up as generative, proactive, successful in creating the relationship you want with your boss or passive, submissive, and resentful? One of the critical success factors for a flourishing career is the ability to relate, negotiate, and work powerfully with a network of key relationships. At the very center of this web of high-leverage relationships is the boss. The different bosses you work with throughout your career will collectively either end up providing you with a set of wings so you can reach the greatest heights or they will accentuate gravity, making it difficult or even impossible for you to reach your aspirations.

These various bosses will exhibit different management and leadership styles, personalities, and philosophies. The ability to adapt and to create a powerful and productive working relationship with bosses in all circumstances is critical to your immediate success, as well as to your progression in the organization and in your career. The problem is that people seldom take into account their own responsibility in that relationship and the opportunity they have to shape it to their advantage.

> *Indulging yourself in old conversations—"my boss is a jerk," "she doesn't listen," "he just dominates"—keeps you trapped in the vicious circle.*

We all recognize that our boss has the power to fire, demote, or promote us, and to give us a great or mediocre score in our yearly performance assessment. In other words, to help us create a new future. Thus we often tend to become passive and submissive in our relationship, sometimes to the point of being victims. When we are in victim mode, we tend to complain: "My boss is changing directions all the time, is so unpredictable and impossible to work with," "My boss micromanages me," "My boss doesn't trust me," "My boss has no people skills," "My boss doesn't acknowledge the progress we have made," and the list goes on. If in those moments, you stop and listen to your own voice, do you think that you speak like a powerful human being in a leadership role?

The truth is that most people automatically go into a reactive mode in their relationship with the boss as opposed to intentionally embracing a generative approach. They do this naturally, effortlessly, and mostly unconsciously, no matter who the boss is and how the boss behaves. This shows up as you trying to protect yourself, avoiding losing, being pleasing and defensive. We all play the same racket, like a conspiracy of the weak.

> *Generate a new conversation: "I stand for my boss's success," "I will provide what the boss needs," "I will sell my proposal by speaking to my boss's listening."*

The alternative is to shift the paradigm 180 degrees. You can choose to be accountable, generative, intentional, and committed. You can embrace the boss you have complete with strengths and faults, and choose to generate a relationship where the company, the boss, and you yourself will be empowered and successful. You can silence the internal dialogue of negativity and choose to generate a powerful conversation in which both can succeed together: "I stand for my boss's success," "I will give him what he needs," "I will sell my proposal by speaking to her listening."

TEMPLATE FOR ACTION

1. *Align yourself to and stand for your boss's success.* Your success and your boss's success are intricately related. You are both on the same team. Ask yourself, "How can I make

my boss successful?" and "How can I contribute?" Hold yourself responsible for understanding and providing it. "Walk in your boss's moccasins" and truly understand the priorities, expectations, needs, and concerns of the boss's job, and be proactive in acting consistent with them. To help you identify your boss's mindset, gain clarity about the following questions:

What is the boss's vision for the business and why?

What are the boss's drivers and why?

What are the boss's expectations for the team that you are part of and for you specifically?

What matters most for your boss? What are the boss's biggest concerns?

If you cannot answer these questions with clarity or if you have some assumptions or partial ideas but are not sure, ask for a meeting with your boss and have a dialogue with the intent to become completely clear about them. Your objective is to generate understanding and alignment with your boss. See if you can own your boss and your boss's commitments as a result of this conversation.

2. *Stand for your boss's contributing to your own success by setting up a coaching relationship.* Make some extraordinary commitments to the business and ask your boss to meet frequently (once a month for ninety minutes or so) as a thinking partner and coach. Prepare each coaching session. Identify current issues, dilemmas, and breakdowns, and send e-mail to your boss twenty-four hours before the session to describe what you want to discuss. Come to the session prepared to present an honest (not defensive) summary of where you are in regard to your breakthrough commitments. Make some specific requests for coaching regarding your issues and dilemmas. Be open and forthcoming with issues.

3. *For smooth sailing in the relationship, be aware of what triggers the boss's reactions and act accordingly.* Ask yourself: What doesn't work? For example: late starts to meetings, not being in communication enough, or bringing too many small issues that you should solve yourself. Then ask: What works? What does your boss need to be empowered? Most of those things you can easily provide with a little time and effort. Mostly it requires thoughtfulness.

4. *Be a good thinking partner.* Be committed to getting the deeper issues on the table. Be a great listener for the opposing views. Ask

questions to deepen your understanding of your boss's position. Make sure your boss is heard. At the same time, be a strong advocate for your own point of view. Prepare yourself to present your position with clarity and with the support of potent examples and data. Be patient and stay with it until you also feel heard. Don't lose your temper, even internally.

5. *Prepare yourself for all meetings with your boss, whether within a group or one-on-one.* Whether you lead the meeting or not, prepare yourself. When your boss is leading the meeting, make sure you know the purpose and intended results and who is participating. Identify what you want to get out of the meeting and what you intend to contribute. When you are leading the meeting, create the purpose and intended results, communicate them in advance, and try to understand your boss's issues and concerns coming into the meeting so that you can own them, and you can speak to the boss's listening.

6. *Turn your complaints into requests.* Avoid turning your complaints into hall gossip. Behind every complaint there is a commitment and a request to make. So get clear on what is not working for you, what your specific request is, and go talk to your boss.

Chapter 20

Create an Extraordinary Career in a Turbulent World

Go for Mastery, Not Competence

SITUATION: You have noticed lately that once-safe mid-management jobs are being replaced by microchips or farmed out to Pakistan, South Korea, and Mexico. How can you increase your chances of success in a Fortune 500 firm or survive as a free agent? *Now hear this!*

Robert in a Coaching Conversation with a High-Tech Manager

Red Doer, a business unit manager for a high-tech company, was good at performing and at mastering the political chessboard, especially by managing up to his boss Rick Rogers, the CEO, a companion on many fishing trips. However, there was a buzz in the organization about Red that as a general manager, he was good at setting goals but had an enormous appetite for planning everything out in detail and a taste for micromanaging people as well. To Red's dismay (and his boss's), this buzz was getting stronger all the time and we were brought in to coach him on a remedial basis. His boss told me, "It's a leadership issue."

We did some 360-degree interviews, and during these conversations, people uniformly agreed that Red would never be a natural leader of a large organization. It also emerged that, while Red might eventually become a competent leader, he had the potential to become a top negotiator for the company. "He is way beyond competent as a negotiator," one person said, "a virtuoso at least, and sometimes truly masterful."

I went to Red with this feedback and said, "I think you are at a fork in the road and the direction you take will determine whether you have an ordinary or extraordinary career from this point on. You can take the beaten path and focus on improving your leadership competence and perhaps rise up the hierarchy. Or you can take a less-traveled road where you have already demonstrated occasional mastery."

Rick's response was, "You gotta be kidding. I've spent almost twenty years clawing my way up to my present position, which is a point of pride for me. Now you are asking me to opt out and consider a whole new career direction—in a staff job, yet. I don't get it."

I said to Red, "There is an old Indian saying that, if you don't change the direction you are headed, you are likely to wind up where you are going. If you stay on the general management track, you can, with the help of coaching, manage to stay at the same level you are on now, but I seriously doubt whether you will climb higher. Also there is a chance you will be moved out to make room for rising stars."

I continued, "I happen to know from conversations with Rick that there is a vice president slot open in charge of strategic acquisitions, where your mastery in negotiation skills can come into play. As you know, growth by acquisition is considered a high priority for the company in the next few years. I think this is a chance to shift your weight to the opposite foot and take your next step into a field that could result in an extraordinary career and give you more career mobility should you decide to leave."

Red said, "I guess I am a product of this company, which is damned hierarchal, and gauging my career path and value accordingly. To be perfectly candid, I have been doing anything I could to climb up the ladder, even taking on jobs I couldn't stand. Now you are telling me to turn my back on all that and start a whole new career. It does sound good to think of reaching mastery on a new playing field instead competence on my old one. Maybe I could make a powerful contribution that way. . . . I have to think about this for a few days."

 TEACHABLE POINT OF VIEW: The game is mastery, not competence.

Think about it. The most successful people in any field never settle for competency; they go for mastery at something they love that also has economic value. The result: they wind up spending more of their working hours doing what they love, dominating their profession, and making a hell of a lot of money.

Tiger Woods's goal isn't competence; it is mastery. Robert DeNiro doesn't just try to deliver a competent performance; what he wants is a masterful one. When the batters step up to the plate, Pedro Martinez of the Red Sox seeks to be a master pitcher, not just to go out there and put in a day's work. Finally, if leadership is an art, according to John Byrne of *BusinessWeek,* then Jack Welch is a master painter, not merely a competent CEO.[1]

> *Whether you work in a Fortune 500 company or the Free Agent Nation, your chances of being a hot, sought-after talent are much higher if you are masterful, rather than just competent.*

The real issue, as Tom Peters says, is that if you want to have a stellar career based on a "Brand You World" and a hot company, it isn't about plain vanilla competencies, it is about mastery. It used to be easy to hide out as a white-collar slave in a Fortune 500 firm's cubicle farm, secure in your job as a "competent" software engineer, bean counter, call center manager.

In today's world economy, with webified companies, these white-collar jobs can be as competently performed by an employee sitting in Ghana, Pakistan, or South Korea as they can by someone sitting in Boston, Houston, or Silicon Valley. Today and in the future, whether you work in a "White Collar Tower" or the "Free Agent Nation," the only chance you have of being a sought-after talent and pulling down the big bucks is being able to do something creative, innovative, and radical and do it with mastery.

The culture of settling for mere competence suited the Fortune 500 company of the 1960s, where the word *talent* was rarely used and workers were seen as replaceable parts in the productivity process. It fit well in the business culture of the 1980s, where competitive advantage meant having a few "core competencies" and some run-of-the-mill employees who focused on total quality and continuous improvement. In the 1990s, *competencies* became a human resource term applied in job selection and management development programs.

It has been our observation that when you pick a starting pitcher on a baseball team or starting point guard on a basketball team, you go on a talent quest to find someone who has mastery, someone who can be a "franchise player." Yet in business, the people who pick starting leaders for CEO jobs, business unit managers, or department heads often settle for mere competence.

One thing is certain, in a world where global competition increases every day, where no enterprise is insulated from the relentless forces of the marketplace, and where nanotechnology, biotechnology, and innovation promise to transform industries overnight, the culture of competence is not enough. Company leaders are increasingly going to have to transform their culture and create a culture of mastery, while at the same time actively exploring creative, innovative, weird ways of doing things.

> *To achieve mastery, make your passion your work, doing*
> *everything with a 100 percent commitment to excellence.*
> *Go for extraordinary results no matter what.*

Today every company that we do coaching in has a list of so-called competencies that they expect individuals to match up with. And these competencies are supposedly linked to the strategy. The fact is, as good as this idea seems, it is generally a lot of hokum, because in most companies, if you ask the average chief executive, vice president, team leader, or computer guy what the competencies are, they will smile and sheepishly say something like, "Truthfully, for the life of me, I can't remember."

We usually tell people that it's okay to have a list of competencies linked to your strategic imperatives, as long as you don't take it too seriously. In truth, it is our belief that these long and boring lists of skills and capabilities are not suited to the virtual economy of today, where only 10 percent of all workers work as managers in Fortune 500 companies.[2] Dramatic change is the order of the day, and tinkering isn't enough. Today we need a special kind of employee, someone who can deliver something really extraordinary.

If you are merely competent, you might wind up at best as the general manager of an irrelevant business unit in a white-collar company, a bean counter and cubicle slave in the finance department, a trainer in the human resource department teaching fundamental communications skills, or one of hundreds of IT people in the bowels of your organization programming computer code.

> *Mastery involves an exquisite level of attention.*

Mastery at something—anything—however, might get you the chief executive's job of a really cool company, the lead finance role on a fascinating and intriguing deal, the IT lead on a secret next-generation Internet project, or a spot as chief guru of an organization's cultural transformation. If you want a cream-of-the-crop job in a big company, or if you want to have the real option to leave and go do something else, then make the decision right now to find out where your passions and talents lie and what work you love to do, and make a decision to become master of the house.

Mastery means not only being excellent at what you do but being able to jump into hot projects, set very high goals and standards, and crack problems that look difficult or impossible to the average competent worker. It means not only coming up with creative, innovative solutions but executing to the nth degree, paying attention to details others would ignore, and having the whole thing turn out exactly, perfectly, and aesthetically.

TEMPLATE FOR ACTION

1. *Stop taking any old job just because it's a step up the ladder.* Most traditional organizations are modeled after a Napoleonic hierarchy where people click their heels, salute, and take any job in order to get a another rung up the ladder. This tends to result in people's ignoring their true passions, talents, and gifts, and winding up in a career that is anything but extraordinary. Instead of thinking vertically, think horizontally, in terms of specific skills or capabilities you would like to develop an extraordinary career around: negotiating big deals, doing research and development, designing new technology, reinventing the supply chain, coming up with advertising campaigns, or pitching to big customers.

2. *Decide on an area where you want to achieve mastery based on the principle of "distinct or extinct."* Launching an extraordinary career starts with figuring out what you can do with some degree of mastery that is powerful and distinct. If you just learn to master a middle management job that can be exported to India, China, or Thailand or that a computer chip will eventually be able to do, the chances are that you will become extinct. What are you passionate about at work? What powerful and distinct contribution can you make? What specific kinds of tasks can you honestly say you do with mastery or at least

come close? How could you better leverage that into a brand new you and jump-start your career?

3. *Set sky-high standards for yourself and others.* Every time we send masterful coaches out on assignment, it's clear they are expected to perform with mastery, not competence. This allows us to distinguish our brand and really deliver for our clients. How about you? When you go to your job or join a hot project, do you set high standards and expect masterful performance from yourself and others or merely expect people to deliver average results?

4. *In mastering something, figure out where you are on the learning curve.* Think not about the strategy of your organization or the theory of work but about the actual work you want be masterful at. Then figure out where you are in regard to the "seven levels of mastery": (1) master, (2) virtuoso, (3) competent worker, (4) advanced beginner, (5) beginner, (6) bull in a china shop, (7) jerk. It helps enormously if you have someone who is a role model whose skills, attitudes, and results you can use as a benchmark. Look at strengths and areas for development. When you are in a project, spend at least 80 percent of your time doing, 20 percent learning by reading, talking, reflecting.

5. *Find a thinking partner.* Taking on a big job or world-changing project can be an exciting experience at first. Then there is the inevitable crash when you discover, as Einstein said, that the same level of thinking that got you into the problem will never be sufficient to get you out of it. See if you can find a thinking partner who can help you come up with solutions that everyone will later say were a masterstroke. The role of the thinking partner is to listen to understand the situation, ask probing and provocative questions that surface, challenge, and shift the basis of your reasoning, and brainstorm creative solutions.

6. *Do everything with a commitment to excellence, paying 100 percent attention to detail.* Most people do 85 percent of a job with excellence and then do the other part with an attitude of "good enough is good enough." Mastery is about doing the whole job with a commitment to excellence, paying attention to the last meaningful detail.

7. *Drive for completion in the face of obstacles, hurdles, and roadblocks.* Sometimes people we are coaching habitually leave projects uncompleted and let deadlines stretch out ad nauseam. Challenged

on this, they tend to reply, "It's in process," and then talk about the stumbling blocks they face. Our standard answer to that is, "Look, when you are up to something big, what the hell do you expect beside stumbling blocks?" Mastery doesn't mean sitting down on the side of the road when this happens. It means driving the project to completion, as well as involving yourself in rigorous, active inquiry into a breakthrough solution that will make these stumbling blocks disappear.

8. *The acid test of mastery is producing extraordinary results, no matter what, and doing it with aesthetics.* Peek underneath the hood of a Ford Thunderbird; look at the design of an Apple iMac or at the layout of Marks & Spencer's new supply chain. The sometimes weird people—like J. Mays of Ford, Renaldo Bocarti of Apple, or Chris Head of M&S—who create, innovate, and bring about irreversible change don't just do live projects or just solve massive engineering problems, they do it with the skill of a creative artist and with a total appreciation of the aesthetics involved. The aesthetics include not only the technical aspect of the job and the design of the package, but the human process by which you negotiate the chessboard. Read about Mays, Bocarti, Head. Read the bios on the political mastery of Lorenzo de Medici, Gandhi, and FDR. Make whatever you do (human or technical) beautiful, something you can stand back and admire for its aesthetics.

Chapter 21

Dealing With Derailers

Shine Your Light, Manage Your Darker Side

SITUATION: You've read that the average tenure of Fortune 500 CEOs is 2.7 years. Like you, most of these guys learned how to leverage their strengths. Yet they didn't ask for feedback on their gaps that would cause them to derail. *Don't make the same mistake.*

Robert in a Coaching Conversation with a Biotech Executive

Lee was in her own words a CAP (a Chinese American Princess) whose family had sacrificed everything to send her to MIT School of Molecular Biology and then to the Stanford Business School for an MBA. She had been written up by *Fortune* as part of breed of super-smart, sophisticated, and stylish "high-flying" female executives that were taking the new biotechnology industry by storm. Lee said to me with dismay, "The date of the article was three and one half years ago. I have been a totally dedicated employee of Genex and delivered results, but the number of promotions I have received have slowed down dramatically since then."

She called me in for a powwow after the chairman came to her one day and told her she was not a shoe-in for the job of the next COO. "You are highly qualified for the job, but you have some things that are getting in your way and perhaps coaching could help," he had told her. The first time I spoke with Lee, I told her that any career derailers probably had more to do with who she was being on the job than with what she knew or what she was doing. I asked, "Are you being inspiring or demotivating, humble or arrogant, gracious or petty, trusting or habitually suspicious? It is who you are being that shapes your perceptions, your thinking and behavior, and how you show up in the organization for others. Let me get some 360-degree feedback to get some insight into what's going on."

I thought about how to set the stage for her listening to the 360-degree feedback I was about to give, which I believed might be hard to take. To do this I began the session by reading a section of the Zanders' book, *The Art of Possibility: Transforming Professional and Personal Life*.[1] The section talked about the two fundamentally different commitments in life, which manifest as a way of being. The first is a commitment to succeed by getting to the top of a pile of bodies (being right and making others wrong). The alternative possibility is to live your life as a commitment to being a contribution. Lee was very inspired by this and told me, "All I want to do is be a contribution."

"I am glad you appreciate that, Lee. And having said that, I need to tell the truth, because today you are showing up as full of blind ambition, not a contribution, and there is a negative conversation swirling in the hallways as a result." We went over some of the feedback verbatim: "Lee is very smart and ambitious, but doesn't care about other people's success." "From day one at Genex, she's been brilliant at solving business problems, but as her confidence grew, her brilliance turned into arrogance and this is now a significant derailer." "In meetings with her team Lee holds forth on her brilliant ideas in a dominating way and belittles anyone who disagrees, giving them a cold stare." One of her peers told me that when he had said, "You seem to be very certain that you are right," Lee's response was, "That's because I am."

Some of the feedback was tough to take and Lee's eyes welled up. "I've tried to do everything right as a leader, and not only do I not get a promotion, I get this feedback."

"Lee, the reason you didn't get the promotion is because of a certain way of thinking and the behavior that comes from it. Of course," I added sympathetically, knowing that Lee had been shaken by the feedback, "everything here is transformable. The question is, Lee, are you ready to transform your behavior and do you want my help in doing so?"

She readily agreed. "Just how do we go about doing that?"

TEACHABLE POINT OF VIEW: In danger of derailing? Shine light on your strengths; don't let your darker side take over.

> *Most leaders play to the same one or two strengths,*
> *but they are unaware of their derailers, and unaware*
> *that they are unaware.*

The first thing we know about leaders is that they are usually people with vision and high moral principles who initiate change and are competent at some aspect of the business. The second thing we know about leaders is that at least two-thirds fail in their careers, usually due to derailers—the darker side of their leadership makeup (or their dysfunctional behavior). The third thing we know about leaders is that they often get an inadequate level of confrontation and feedback about these behaviors. Experience shows that when leaders get feedback about their derailers, they can learn to recognize and disperse them and thus increase their chances of success.

> *We suggest you get some 360-degree feedback to find out*
> *what your potential derailers are and then create a*
> *personal development plan.*

Industrial psychologist Paul Hogan has written that most leaders have strengths but also have one or more derailers. The strength represents the front and the derailer often represents the back. And the bigger the front, the bigger the back. For example, in Lee's story, the derailer's front is "brilliance" and the back is a tendency toward arrogance. In the same sense, strong analytical skills can lead to identifying risks and on the other hand lead to excessive caution.

It is important to not just recognize what your derailers are but also to get to their source and then consciously and intentionally shift them. This might involve calling in a professional coach or psychologist and talking about the specific instances where you exhibited attitudes or behaviors that might cause you to derail. The psychologist's role is to ask questions intended to get at motivations you are not aware of: "What was your intention at that meeting?" "What were you trying to prove by controlling everything people did?" "How do you feel about yourself when you think back on those incidents?"

Find a "Deputy Coach" and Ask "How Am I Doing?"

If you are dealing with some derailers of any consequence, a good idea might be to find a coach who can give you insight and feedback on an ongoing basis as you work to shift your attitudes or behavior. Yet since a professional coach cannot be in your workplace all the time, we often suggest that people appoint a "deputy coach"— someone who is close at hand and can provide feedback on a day-in, day-out basis as needed.

TEMPLATE FOR ACTION

1. *Discover your derailers.* Which of these derailers could be yours?

Arrogance—you like being right and making others wrong.

People pleaser—you are out to look good.

Dr. Jekyll and Mr. Hyde syndrome—you are prone to mood swings.

Excessive caution—you are reluctant to make decisions.

Chronic distrust—you are always suspicious.

Aloofness—you don't show your human side.

Mischievousness—the rules are meant for others, not for you.

Eccentricity—you refuse to conform for the sake of it.

Malicious obedience—you say one thing, do another, and undermine authority.

Perfectionism—you spend so much time getting things perfect that you don't complete anything.

Melodrama—you always have a dramatic story about what happened to you and how "they are doing it"

2. *Get some 360-degree feedback on derailing behaviors.* Ask someone to conduct a round of 360-degree feedback interviews for you, asking people what you are doing that drives them up the wall, what you are doing that gets you in trouble, and what you are doing that may lead you to derail in your career.

3. *Take 100 percent responsibility for anything you did that resulted in negative conversations about you.* If others tend to be aggravated with you or some of your behaviors and this has resulted in a negative impression about you in the company, recognize that you have a real problem; don't blame others or create a story about how you are right and they are wrong.

4. *Consciously and intentionally decide to transform your behavior and generate a new conversation about yourself.* This should be a conversation that allows your career to take off rather than fall flat. It starts with declaring new ways of being and giving up old ways of being: "I am committed to the possibility of [achieving something you want]. I am committed to giving up [the behaviors that are getting in the way].

5. *Learn to recognize the stressful situations that trigger derailing behaviors and to keep your darker side from taking over.* Create a short list of the derailers you have. Then next to each one write down the kinds of people, stressful situations, and events that tend to trigger derailing behaviors. The next time you are in the situation, resist the impulse to allow your darker side to determine who you will be in the matter.

6. *Learn from examples.* Ron, a charismatic leader and very confident manager, had earned the nickname "the black cloud." This was due to an automatic tendency to reject new ideas when they were presented to him, before hearing them out. We coached Ron to anticipate the kinds of meetings on his calendar where this was likely to happen and to resist the impulse to revert to form. Instead of categorically rejecting an idea, Ron asked people to clarify their reasoning or data. This led to a healthy form of dialogue and more of a shared understanding about which new ideas would work and which might not.

Chapter 22

There's a Conversation Out There About You That's a Career Wrecker

Publicly Acknowledge It, Take Responsibility for It, Campaign to Change It

SITUATION: You have worked hard to transform your leadership style and derailers, but you've got a rap sheet from the past. Too bad! You may not like it, but the way others perceive you, rightly or wrongly, will shape your career (and your future)! *Here is how to shift those perceptions, one conversation at a time.*

Michel in a Coaching Conversation with a Marketing Leader

I got a call from Dave Severs, a remarkable young executive in his prime. In our nearly two years' work together, I had never heard him sound so discouraged. This high-energy guy with a commitment the size of Texas was ready to quit. A year before, when his company went through a merger, the marketing leader of the other organization was chosen over Dave to head the combined marketing division. Dave felt that he should have been offered the job, given that he had a stronger marketing background and had produced some pretty impressive results, but he swallowed the pill and embraced the choice of the corporation.

It helped that he was given assurances by his new boss that he was going to be the clear number two guy with prospects for a bigger job down the road. But lately, those prospects had not seemed to pan out. One year had passed, and Dave had not been given the much anticipated and well-deserved salary grade-level promotion. Dave felt increasingly that his number two guy status was a farce and that he was at best considered as just another member of the marketing leadership team.

"Michel," Dave sighed, "since the merger I have put my disappointment aside and I have used my energy to deal with the complex task of merging the two marketing organizations. My team has produced significant financial contribution to the bottom line of the corporation, and I have performed beyond expectations. In addition, as you know, I have worked hard and openly to improve some of my leadership gaps—like my tendency to play Lone Ranger, to overreact emotionally to people who were not aligned with my ambitions for the business, and to not provide clear expectations for my organization. I feel that I have now bridged those gaps, yet I don't feel I get the respect I deserve. I am in my prime, and I don't want to stay here and miss the opportunity to play a bigger game. If they don't recognize me, someone else will!"

I suggested to Dave that I conduct some 360-degree feedback interviews to get clarity on how he was perceived today as a leader and what the current leadership issues were that were preventing him from being appreciated by his bosses. I conducted ten interviews, with his boss and some colleagues and direct reports, to gather insights on Dave's leadership. The results of those interviews could hardly have been more positive.

Dave was perceived by all, without exception, as a great boss and a strong leader, and he clearly had earned the respect of everyone working with and for him. In summary, people were raving about his business knowledge, his passion for the business, his integrity, his personal commitment to coach and develop people, and his drive to lead changes into the organization. But the most revealing interview was the one with Mike Haliway, his boss. Mike was extremely impressed by Dave's leadership skills and contribution to the business.

"The truth is that our relationship started on the wrong foot, which was not Dave's fault. When I came into my new role, I was provided with a leadership assessment from senior leaders on each of the people who were joining my leadership team. Today, I am very frustrated with that initial assessment because the negative feedback I got proved to be absolutely wrong."

"For the past few months, I have been fighting for Dave to get the grade-level promotion he so deserves, and for the senior team to consider Dave as my successor. I am frustrated at the resistance I am bumping into. It is clear to me that the senior leaders are carrying an old picture of him and they are holding on to it for dear life, refusing to recognize Dave's progress and transformation."

The next time I met with Dave, I gave him a summary of the feedback, starting with the insightful conversation I had with Mike Haliway. Dave was glad to see that Haliway respected him and that he was fighting on his behalf. He was also shocked and sobered by the lack of visibility for his results and leadership evolution with the senior leadership team.

"Dave," I said, "I think that perhaps it is time to create your own personal campaign to shift those entrenched opinions and to generate a new possibility for yourself as a leader and for your career."

"I'm with you, Michel. Let's get to work."

 TEACHABLE POINT OF VIEW: The conversation that exists about you as leader will be your best friend or worst enemy! Know it, own it, and do something about it.

Nobody in the history of humankind is more equipped than we are to understand the power of perception. We are bombarded every day by smart advertisements that shape how we think about thousands of products. Quality continues to matter, yes—but let's face it, image is everything.

In the same way, people carry an image or perception of each of us that shapes whether they "buy" us or not. The larger our leadership role, the more eyes are on us, and how we are perceived by others has tremendous consequences on what is possible for us, businesswise and careerwise. As leaders, we are on stage all the time, and hundreds or even thousands of people will form opinions about us, usually from short moments of exposure, or from the conversations that they have with others. On the other hand, people who work more closely with us form their own opinions over time and from countless interactions. Their conclusions are often more balanced, as they are based on more data points, but they may also be more unforgiving as they come with the strength of certainty and plenty of evidence.

We call this individual and collective perception the "conversation" about you as a leader. Perception is not the same as truth, and most of us defend ourselves vehemently against what we consider an inaccurate perception. But whether fair or unfair, people's perceptions will always shape their actions—whether that is to give you a raise, offer you a promotion, or follow your lead with trust and action. If you have high aspirations for your business and career, it is imperative that you understand the current conversation that exists about you in the organization, and determine whether that conversation is detrimental to or supportive of what you are trying to achieve.

The conversation that exists about you may actually be extremely empowering for both your business and career aspirations. "If anyone can do this, he is the guy" or "Nobody else could do this but Sally. With her on the project, we will succeed." On the other hand, some conversations are not so conducive to what you are trying to achieve. "He is only here for a short while, only a quick step to bigger things. He doesn't really care, so why should we?"

Identifying the conversation about you and shifting it, if necessary, is crucial if you want to make a difference in your organization or advance your career. When Michael Dell, founder of Dell

Computer, was told in the fall of 2001 through internal interviews that he was impersonal and detached, and as a result, few employees felt a strong loyalty to him or to the company, he took the feedback seriously. He met with his team and acknowledged that he was painfully shy, which made him seem aloof and unapproachable. He vowed to forge tighter bonds with his team. Following that meeting, he showed the videotape of his public declaration to change to every manager in the company—several thousand people. Dell is a great example of someone who realized the consequences of the way he showed up to people in his organization, who listened to the feedback, and who did something drastic and visible to change the organizational conversation about his leadership.

> *You shift people's perceptions of you one conversation at a time, through the quality of your speaking, listening, and action.*

Michael Dell at least had something real to deal with. At times, people's conversation will be based on old impressions of you, taking no account of how you might have changed recently as a leader. In this case you need to take responsibility for how you acted in the past and for not having communicated properly to the right people the results you have produced and the style of leadership you have now adopted. You cannot expect people to change their conversation just because you have changed. As a matter of fact, most people tend to be rather inflexible when it comes to the conversations they have created about others.

At the end of the day, your ability to understand and manage the conversation that exists about you will be critical to the velocity, the ease, and the extent of success. Managing the perceptions of others means generating your own personal campaign to have your leadership and business accomplishments, as well as those of your team, visible to the organization. It is also about having the leadership changes you and your team go through, and the transformation you undertake, be seen and acknowledged by people in the greater organization.

TEMPLATE FOR ACTION

1. *Identify the conversation about you.* Gather specific and insightful feedback on how you show up by asking six to ten people at various levels and positions the following questions. Pick people you know will be straight with you.

How do I come across to you as a leader? How do I come across to others?

What is the story about me? What are people saying and thinking about me as leader?

Is there any event or behavior that is at the heart of people's perceptions? Put your natural and understandable defensiveness aside as you listen, just try to get it. Thank people for being straight.

2. *Consider having someone else interview people around you to get the feedback.* If you are in a high position in the organization and you think people might not say what they really think, or you want a wider or deeper view, have someone from human resources or outside the company (your coach) do 360-degree feedback interviews about you. This person can also help you get to the essence of what people are saying about you.

3. *Decide how you want the conversation to change.* Reflect on the feedback and its implications. Don't be a victim. Take responsibility for the current conversation, understanding your attitudes and behaviors that might have contributed to it. Then look at how you want that conversation to change. What new ways of being, thinking, or acting must you take on? What current ways of being, thinking, or acting do you want to abandon?

4. *Communicate to people that you heard the feedback and that you are committed to making a change.* Speak openly about your past shortcomings and your commitment to change to people who work for you, to your boss, and to any other key individuals, and ask for support and suggestions. Get them on board with you. Solicit regular feedback by asking people how you are doing. You may want to appoint some "deputy coaches" who will intervene when they see you falling back to the old ways. This creates a huge opening for people to reveal their own vulnerabilities and goes a long way toward creating a culture of learning and coaching.

5. *If you have made changes and want the new you to be seen, launch a campaign to change the conversation.* Accomplishments often get lost, so keep an accomplishment journal for yourself. Make the commitments, progress, and accomplishments of your team and organization known and visible to the corporation and to senior leaders. Be proactive in your upward and lateral communication. For example, get an article written and published in the corporate newsletter about the progress and ambition of your business area. Send a brief, well-crafted communication to senior leaders on a quarterly basis to keep them abreast of progress and current challenges.

Chapter 23

Beat Burnout

Get to the Source of Frustration First, Then Deal With Overload

SITUATION: You have a job that gives you an opportunity to make a difference, but all you do is travel and work all the time and it's a body beater. You are extremely frustrated about the petty tyrants, as well as the walls and organizational absurdities. *How do you avoid burning out?*

Robert in a Coaching Conversation with an Executive Opening the American Market for a Japanese Pharmaceutical Company

Aaron Kane is a hard-charging, take-no-prisoners executive in a Japanese pharmaceutical firm that makes generic drugs, as well as a specialty drug for multiple sclerosis. His mission: to launch the company's entry into the U.S. market from scratch—a big career opportunity. He has great passion and drive but he has been working almost eighty hours a week building the finance, marketing, supply chain, and IT departments, while shuttling back and forth to Tokyo for meetings.

He asked me to coach him to be the leader he needed to be to source an extraordinary future for this organization in the United States and to master the corporate chessboard in Japan. This was all a heady experience, but it was taking a toll on his health, well-being, and family. I brought it up in our coaching call, "A start-up operation is fun stuff, but I am concerned that you are a potential burnout case. You have all the symptoms."

Aaron asked what I meant by that, so I pulled down a dictionary from the credenza and read the definition of burnout: "exhaustion of physical or emotional strength or motivation usually as a result of prolonged stress, causing fatigue or frustration." Aaron said, "Yes, Robert, I am very frustrated. First of all, the people in the home office just don't understand how it is here. And second, I have been working from 6 A.M. to 8 P.M. every day and traveling to Japan once a month to participate in meetings where I get very little appreciation for my efforts, and I rarely see my family.

"On top of that, I am expected to keep everyone around here inspired and empowered. I hate to admit this, but the fact is I am going beyond burnout and starting to melt down. I have gained twenty pounds and become a Starbucks addict. I can't keep this up much longer. Do you have any words of advice?"

"It is very clear that, just as you need a strategy of resilience for your organization, you need a strategy of personal resilience for yourself or you will not be able to get where you are going," I responded.

"You are right," he agreed. "Let's focus on that in this call."

TEACHABLE POINT OF VIEW: If you want to source your organization, you have to source yourself first.

A big job can be a heady experience, but it's also a long, hard slog. Designing a strategy of personal resilience that reinvigorates your spirits and supports your health and vitality is essential to reaching your organizational goals and aspirations. It goes hand in hand with designing a strategy of organizational resilience. It is not about indulging yourself, it is about being able to press on.

Designing a strategy of personal resilience starts with telling yourself, "Superman doesn't live here anymore." If you don't design your job so that a mere mortal can do it, you will face the most dire consequences: spiritual and emotional meltdown, physical breakdown—a heart attack or some other collapse—and loss of effectiveness. The quest for personal resilience includes finding the sources of inspiration in the midst of difficulty, finding productive ways of dealing with being stressed, frustrated, and infuriated, and finding ways of dealing with fatigue.

Finding Sources of Inspiration

The idea of inspiring others with an Impossible Future that captures their imagination is great, but remember—you need to be able to keep yourself inspired if you are going to inspire others. Ask yourself what kinds of things inspire you. You have to realize that you can't take blood from a stone.

One idea we often suggest is to read your Source Document (if you have one) once a week to keep you focused on the future you are creating, in the midst of people who try your patience and difficult facts and circumstances that demand your attention. Another thing we do when coaching people is take them to a big sports event to watch top-level play or to visit a great museum like the Louvre in Paris where leaders like Napoleon or Admiral Nelson are depicted in all their glory.

Other sources of inspiration may include reading a biography of a leader like FDR or Gandhi, or Alfred Sloan's *My Life at General*

Motors, going to a big show like *Les Miserables,* or hearing Luciano Pavarotti or Dave Matthews. Or how about watching a great movie. A favorite of mine is *A Gathering Storm,* a PBS special on Winston Churchill that shows how he fought his way back from his "wilderness years" to become prime minister in World War II.

Tell yourself that Superman doesn't live here anymore.
Design your job so that a mere mortal can do it.

Dealing With Exhaustion

The chances are that at some point in your career you will experience burnout as a result of frustration or overload. Let's start with the easy part, overload. One of the first things you need to do to deal with overload is to begin to draw your identity from something other than an action hero. You need a job that a normal human being can do. It is not physically possible for one person to do the work of two to five people on a sustainable basis, even though you would like to believe it is so. In plain terms this means you are going to have to take some things off your plate in the next thirty days.

Next let's talk about your staff. Do you have the right people in the right jobs? Or do you have to come in and pick up the strategy (or whatever) presentation on Friday night before the board meeting on Monday and work all weekend to save the day, thus once again proving you are a hero? The time you spend getting the right people in the right jobs, setting clear goals and expectations, and then coaching them by adding value to their work (not taking work away from them) can be far more valuable than what you spend on your most dramatic rescue mission.

Dealing With Frustration

Overload can be a factor, but in practice burnout is largely caused by frustration. Each of the following five factors can play a significant role:

- *Company ethics you can't live by.* Core values conflicts are deadly. If you see something that reminds you of the next Enron—get out of there fast. If the CEO's or company's values are different from yours when it comes to dealing with people, speak up or clear out.

- A *difficult boss.* This is probably the number one cause of anger and frustration.

    Step 1. Face to face, say you want a better relationship and acknowledge something you admire about your boss.

    Step 2. Clear the air by completing the past, taking responsibility for your part in any breakdowns.

    Step 3. Look at what you can create together going forward.

- A *job or career that doesn't feel right to you.* This can make you feel like you are letting life pass by. Spend some time unearthing your passions and talents with a coach or mentor. Explore interests. Find ways to bring zest factors into your job, or if necessary find a new job.

- *Preoccupation with upsets and anxiety.* Instead of causing yourself undue stress about upsets, step back and take the ten-year view of the situation. What's the worst thing that will happen if this deal doesn't come off? Get someone to be a thinking partner who can help you step back from the upset and see the big picture. Never take other people's behavior personally. There are always more alternatives in a situation than you currently see.

- *Sparse rewards and recognition.* This is a tough one as it makes you feel like your destiny is out of your hands. Give what you want to get by making it a point to praise your boss and other people's efforts. Next, learn to toot your own horn. Each year publish a list of the accomplishments that you and your group have achieved. When you do something you think will please your boss, point it out. "You asked me to improve the Web site and I have." "You asked me to negotiate this deal and it is done."

TEMPLATE FOR ACTION

1. *Ask five people to give you a list of books, movies, plays, and so on that truly inspired them.* Sourcing yourself to source an inspired, high-performing organization starts with putting things in place in your own life that will be a source of inspiration to you as you go through the daily grind. Martin

Luther King Jr. read articles about Gandhi on nonviolent revolution; Gandhi read the works of the American philosopher Henry David Thoreau on civil disobedience. Bill Gates of Microsoft, for example, reads historical biographies of leaders who have made a difference in the world.

2. *Every day, tell yourself, "Superman doesn' t live here anymore."* Take three months of your schedule and label every meeting and activity: makes a difference, is important, or is trivial. Ask a coach or thinking partner to go over this with you. Ask them to challenge you on some of your sacred assumptions. *Does this really make a dif-ference? Or is it only important? Could this activity be dropped or delegated? What are the highest-leverage things to focus on?*

3. *Find out how much vacation time you can take and then take all of it without guilt.* Tell yourself or your secretary not to overbook your calendar. Take thirty minutes in the morning and in the afternoon to do your e-mail. Build in another thirty minutes in the morning or eve-ning for creative reflection. Make a solemn oath to leave work on time and go home. Don't take a lot of work projects home with you. Take inspiring vacations. One of our clients took a three-week vacation to India for his twenty-fifth wedding anniversary. He booked a hotel where he and his wife would wake up on the day of the anniversary looking out the window at the Taj Mahal.

4. *Eat until you are 70 percent full, do exercise with iron discipline, and take power naps.* You have to have a commitment to eat right, exercise, and rest that is bigger than your moods. Make sure you get at least twenty minutes a day of exercise, four days a week. Pick an appointed hour in the day when you run, walk, work out, or whatever, and stick to that regimen with iron discipline whether you feel like it not. Find some time during the day or when you first come home to engage in short naps.

5. *Sit down with your boss and have an honest talk.* The chances are that at the same moment you start thinking that your boss is kind of a jerk, your boss is thinking the very same thing about you. Take your boss out to lunch and talk about how you can have a more productive working relationship. Here's a template for your opening comments: One thing I admire about you is . . . One thing I have difficulty with is . . . One thing I want to create with you is . . .

6. *Don' t take stuff personally.* As coaches we often point out that the boss would have given anyone the same treatment you ran into in that meeting, because, for example, it was a bad hair day. The target just happened to be you. Also become aware of how you hold things in your mind. It's not what happens to you that makes you happy or unhappy, it's what you think it means.

7. *Balance work and family.* Most leaders complain that they never have enough time to spend with their families, and then proceed to stick to the same work schedule, coming up with one excuse after another. One way around this is to have a fixed night once a week to spend with your spouse on a date, and other nights to do something fun or interesting with each of your children.

8. *Have fun!* Create a list of ten things you can do to have fun and make an agreement with yourself and your family to start doing several a week. It doesn't matter much which ones you choose—golf, skiing, sailing, walking, running, shopping, home improvement projects, working on your personal investment portfolio—so long as you genuinely enjoy them and you get some variety.

Chapter 24

Fed Up with Your Job? Take the "Go to America" Attitude and Get Out

Write a Résumé That Is a Ticket to a New and Better Universe

SITUATION: You've spent your career in one company, which feels like the whole universe. Your boss has offered you a choice: stay where you are or take a job that is a side step. *Your masterful coach says you always have more career choices than you can see.*

Robert in a Coaching Conversation with a Manufacturing Company Vice President

Jillian James is a vice president of Airtrain, a large aircraft manufacturer. She has bright blue eyes and a shining record of accomplishment that has rocketed her up the corporate ladder. She has managed the marketing department, new product development, and more recently the P&L of several businesses. She has won the company's "Inspirational Leadership Award" for playing a very significant role in designing coaching programs to develop the "next generation of leaders."

This is why she was put in charge of the Euro Flight Division eighteen months ago. Her work in this division involved developing the A14, a sophisticated commercial airplane employing many emerging technologies and nicknamed the "Golden Goose." Soon after getting into the job, she discovered the truth of the old maxim about all that glitters not being gold, and she began to think about what happened to the golden goose in the story. The A14 project was eating up shocking amounts of capital, coping with costly delays and new technology that was barely off the drawing boards, and it had no clear customers.

"We've got a new CEO at the company," she told me on a coaching call, "Pierre LaFrance. He's looked at the numbers of the Euro Division, scrutinized the budget of the A14, and last week he called me to ask if we had an exit plan to shut the project down. 'Even high flyers make mistakes,' he told me." Shut it down she did, but she began to have the feeling that what happened had sown doubt about her in LaFrance's eyes, and her once soaring career stock appeared to take a slide. She said to me, "I am beginning to wonder if there is another—newer and better—universe out there somewhere."

I replied, "Jillian, I think it's time to step back from the front line and the heat of the action and assess your career goals and aspirations, as well as your current situation. We can talk about how to play out your game on the Airtrain corporate chessboard later. At this point, however, I think you need to get that you do have choices. One of the best ways to find this out is to begin to re-imagine yourself in another kind of job in another kind of enterprise, and then design a résumé that will get you an interview."

TEACHABLE POINT OF VIEW: Fed up with your job or company? Take the "Go to America" attitude and write a résumé that gets you an interview and lands you in a new and better universe.

You do have choices!

One of the most frequent issues we face as executive coaches is the need to advise people who feel pissed off with their boss, job, or career. At the same time, these people often act like their company is the entire known universe, with nothing beyond it except sea monsters and dragons. They cling to the security of their little white-collar world, even though they know that in doing so they are forfeiting the possibility of creating a new future. In time, they go from being pissed off to frustrated and profoundly resigned.

We are here to tell you that that there are always more possibilities for an extraordinary life than you currently see. It is possible to take action that lands you in a new and better universe, one loaded with possibilities and opportunities. We often tell our coaching clients, "Why don't you take the 'Let's go to America' attitude like your great-grandparents did when they came to this country from England, France, Germany, Russia, China, or wherever?"

Your ancestors heard about the United States and had the courage and commitment to pack their bags and go, leaving whatever security they had behind them. The idea was that they could leave the tyrannical landed gentry behind them. They could leave the preindustrial village behind them. They could leave the toil of the farm behind them. When they left they came with the possibility of a better life, not with a guarantee of lifetime employment, yearly paid bonuses, and good health benefits. In a way they were all entrepreneurs—whether their business was fishing, farming, or more recently high-tech.

So how about you? If you have known for a long time in your heart of hearts that you are no longer in the right place, why not take the "Go to America" attitude and go someplace else. The main thing that it takes is the courage and commitment to act on your gut instincts, together with the willingness to imagine yourself in a new situation that would allow you to leverage your passions and talents, and to be a much better fit. Instead of viewing yourself as your job, view yourself as the brand new you, with your own unique selling proposition (your USP; what you can do that is uniquely you), and start advertising yourself today.

TEMPLATE FOR ACTION

1. *Build a personal group who can help you match your talents and gifts to a new career.* Make a list of experienced colleagues and friends you have known for years. Contact them and ask them to be part of your "mastermind" group. Tell them your view of your talents, passions, and people preferences, then ask them for some honest feedback as to whether they see you differently. Ask them to be a sounding board for job objectives and companies you have in mind, as well as to brainstorm with you to come up with possibilities you have not discovered.

2. *Come up with a USP based on the brand new you.* Write a sentence or at most a short paragraph that says who you are and what value you provide, perhaps claiming the mantle of leadership (this is your unique selling proposition or USP). For example, at Masterful Coaching, we claim we are the world leaders in executive coaching. In all candor, we feel we are the thought leaders in executive coaching based on some of our paradigm-smashing ideas. We are claiming by way of this USP that we are also one of the biggest and best firms in this area of expertise. Think about an area where you can establish a USP based on claiming the mantle of leadership—for example, Mr. Project, Ms. Creator, and so on.

3. *Create a wide range of career options by spending some time on Google.* Charles Handy talks about two different kinds of companies to get jobs with—the "elephants" and the "fleas."[1] Elephants are big companies like the Fortune 500. Fleas are small companies that feed off these, like professional service firms of various kinds. It turns out that only 10 percent of the workforce in the United States work as managers for one of the elephants. An increasing number of people are starting their own businesses and experiencing the joys and pains of being a flea. A good way to figure out your career options is to go on the Internet to Google and type in subject areas you are interested in—Fortune 500 job postings, restaurant franchises, adventure travel. You can come up with an amazing range of options in three thirty-minute sessions.

4. *Create a written job search plan.* Planning drives action. Develop a specific list of targeted companies, making use of your research, search firms that have previously contacted you, outplacement companies, or colleagues and friends. Create a step-by-step timetable for reaching out and contacting these people, and recruit a committed listener who will hold you accountable to this. "I will contact three companies every day." In the meantime, if you are striking out into new areas, it may be useful to read up on the specialties or companies that are relevant. Again, the Internet is not only information rich, it is also the cheapest printing press in the world.

5. *Create a résumé that's an advertisement to get an interview, not a postmortem on your career.* A great résumé has three main aspects:

A job objective that makes a great promise. Write a headline from a "you" point of view (employer), rather than from a "me" point of view (job hunter). For example, "My job objective is to be a VP of marketing in a company that needs a proven leader who can work with a team to take a product from concept to market." A job objective that comes from a "me" point of view would be more like this: "Seeks Marketing Director position with six-figure salary and stock options."

A skills and accomplishments section that builds the case. Explain why your job objective is something that you can deliver on without breaking a sweat. Apply this by writing one sentence about your skills and then three to five bullets that highlight your greatest accomplishments.

A chronological list of your career experiences. Use bullets to designate key jobs you have held and begin each one with a verb that says something that you did.

6. *Write a cover letter to go with your résumé.* Your cover letter should say something about your job objective and how it meets the company's needs, and if possible about the ones who referred you to the company. "I was speaking to Jack Jeffrey, VP of Finance, and he suggested I send my résumé to you. I am looking for a Senior Marketing position for a company that needs . . . "

7. *Keep in mind that someone you know may know the person you want to read your résumé—or know someone that person knows.* The person who you want to read your résumé and get an interview with may only be 3.5 handshakes away. It is important to tell your story and sell yourself to everyone in your personal network, and pass out

copies of your presentation materials. Get your résumé into the hands of "someone who knows someone" and ask them to hand-deliver it. This takes a little effort, but can pay off big time. If you need to mail your presentation, remember that in today's electronic world e-mail has become the preferred way of sending a résumé or cover letter. Perhaps e-mail is less impressive than embossed stationery, but it makes it much easier for people in interested companies to forward your résumé to others.

8. *For interviews, prepare, rehearse, and prepare some more.* Ask someone in your mastermind group to spend an hour or so with you preparing for an interview. Write down a list of the key questions you think you will be asked, then find a thinking partner to role-play them with you. Give each question your best shot for one to two minutes, and then ask for feedback. To make the preparation process more interesting, try reversing roles. You ask the questions and your thinking partner gives the answers. This can lead to new insights, both in what to say and how to say it.

Notes

Overall

We have changed the names of the people and their companies in the scenarios and other examples throughout the book to protect the confidentiality of our coaching relationships.

Preface

1. Robert Gandossy and Marc Effron, *Leading the Way* (New York: Wiley, 2003).

Introduction

1. The statement from Connie Chung was taken from quotes compiled on www.cybernation.com.

Part One

1. From Teddy Roosevelt's statement, "The credit belongs to the man who is actually in the arena, whose face is marred by dust and sweat and blood; who strives valiantly; who errs and comes short again and again; who knows the great enthusiasms, the great devotions; who spends himself in a worthy cause." Quoted on www.cybernation.com.

2. The story about the strong cultural context created by George Merck II for his company is based on an article by Jim Collins, "The 10 Greatest CEOs of All Time," *Fortune Magazine,* July 7, 2003.

3. The idea of "strategic resilience" is from Gary Hamel, chairman of Strategos; it is discussed on www.strategos.com; see also Hamel's book *Leading the Revolution: How to Thrive in Turbulent Times by Making Innovation a Way of Life* (New York: Plume, 2002).

4. Larry Bossidy writes about the importance of the "People Process" in his book, written with Ram Charan, *Execution: The Discipline of Getting Things Done* (New York: Crown Business, 2002).

Chapter 4

1. The story about General Robert Wood Johnson of Johnson & Johnson is based on an article by Jim Collins, "The 10 Greatest CEOs of All Time," *Fortune Magazine*, July 7, 2003.
2. I am grateful for conversations with Joan Holmes of the Hunger Project. Some of the key ideas presented in this book, for example, "strategic planning in action," are the work of those involved with the Hunger Project. The Hunger Project is a global, strategic organization committed to the sustainable end of world hunger. See Web site: www.hungerproject.org

Chapter 7

1. The story of Grossman at IBM is from Gary Hamel, *Leading the Revolution* (Boston: Harvard Business School Press, 2000).
2. I heard the story about Bob Kraft on sports talk radio on Boston, Massachusetts.

Chapter 8

1. Richard Branson, *Losing My Virginity: How I Survived, Had Fun, and Made a Fortune Doing Business My Way* (New York: Three Rivers Press, 1999).

Part Two

1. The story of Bill Allen at Boeing is based on an article by Jim Collins, "The 10 Greatest CEOs of All Time," *Fortune Magazine*, July 7, 2003.
2. Peter Block, *Stewardship: Choosing Service over Self-Interest* (San Francisco: Berrett-Koehler, 1996).
3. James McGregor Burns writes about FDR in *Transforming Leadership: The Pursuit of Happiness* (Boston: Atlantic Monthly Press, 2003). McGregor Burns's work has had a huge impact on our thinking about leadership.
4. The story of David Packard of Hewlett Packard is based on an article by Jim Collins, "The 10 Greatest CEOs of All Time," *Fortune Magazine*, July 7, 2003.
5. I (Robert) appreciate conversations with James McGregor Burns at the Renaissance Weekend in March 2003. Besides *Transforming Leadership*, his books include *Leadership* (New York: HarperCollins, 1978).
6. The story of David Maxwell of Fannie Mae is based on an article by Jim Collins, "The 10 Greatest CEOs of All Time," *Fortune Magazine*, July 7, 2003.

7. The story about General Robert Wood Johnson of J & J is based on an article by Jim Collins, "The 10 Greatest CEOs of All Time," *Fortune Magazine,* July 7, 2003.

Chapter 10

1. The story about Katherine Graham of the Washington Post Co. is based on an article by Jim Collins, "The 10 Greatest CEOs of All Time," *Fortune Magazine,* July 7, 2003.

Chapter 11

1. The story of Charles Coffin of General Electric is based on an article by Jim Collins, "The 10 Greatest CEOs of All Time," *Fortune Magazine,* July 7, 2003.
2. The story about Jeff Immelt was from an article by Jerry Useem, "It's All Yours Jeff. Now What?" at Fortune.com.
3. The story about David Olgilvy is from Tom Peters, *Re-Imagine* (New York: Dorling Kindersley, 2003).

Chapter 12

1. The story about John F. Kennedy is from a PBS series, *American Experience: The Kennedys.*

Chapter 14

1. You can read about the A player system put into place by Jack Welch at General Electric in his book with John A. Byrne, *Jack: Straight from the Gut* (New York: Warner Books, 2001).

Part Three

1. The story about Warren Buffett comes from a book by Richard Smith and James M. Citrin, *The 5 Patterns of Extraordinary Careers: The Guide for Achieving Success and Satisfaction* (New York: Crown Business, 2003).
2. Daniel Pink, *Free Agent Nation: The Future of Working for Yourself* (New York: Warner Books, 2002).

Chapter 18

1. Harriet Rubin, "Desperately Seeking Vernon," *Fast Company,* August 2002.
2. Albert-Laszlo Barabasi, *Linked: The New Science of Networks* (New York: Perseus, 2002).

Chapter 20

1. John Byrne, "How Jack Welch Runs GE," *BusinessWeek,* June 8, 1998.
2. Tom Peters, *Re-Imagine!* (New York: DK Publishing, 2003).

Chapter 21

1. Benjamin Zander and Rosamund Stone Zander, *The Art of Possibility: Transforming Professional and Personal Life* (Boston: Harvard Business School Press, 2000).

Chapter 24

1. Charles Handy, *The Elephant and the Flea* (Boston: Harvard Business School Press, 2002).

Glossary of Concepts

Breakthrough Projects: The number of people with staid Fortune 500 line jobs where they do the same thing better, year after year, is decreasing. What is increasing is the number of people who come together as individuals or free agents around breakthrough projects that have transformational potential. In many cases, the Impossible Future and the significant business challenge that falls out of it may look less like the goals people set every year and send to corporate headquarters, and more like hot projects that intrigue, fascinate, and get people to give their best.

Coaching: A coach is someone who stands in your greatness and impacts your vision and values. Coaching takes place in the domain of accomplishment, not therapy. Coaching requires being a grounded observer of people as they make a committed attempt to perform, and providing meaningful feedback that allows them to correct their mistakes and produce the desired results for the first time. Coaching involves bringing about a shift in *what people need to do* and *who they need to be* to achieve desired results.

Corporate Chessboard: The closer you get to the top the greater is the competition for powerful positions and resources. Being successful is not just a matter of coming up with a goal and a straightforward and logical plan, it requires embracing the political nature of all organizations. It involves looking at the configuration of kings, queens, knights, and pawns and seeing who you have to strategically influence. It involves campaigning for your ideas as well as building coalitions that increase support and diminish opposition with respect to the different players on the chessboard.

Derailer: People are aware of their leadership strengths and development needs, but often unaware of derailers that might wreck their career. For example, ethical issues, arrogance, aloofness or emotional volatility, having too many blue-sky ideas, or being risk averse. Dealing with derailers involves getting feedback on strengths and problem behavior, and then creating coaching and action strategies to deal with them.

Doing a "What's So" (Facing Reality): At Masterful Coaching we have a Strategic Planning in Action Process that involves setting goals, doing a "What's So," and discovering what's missing that will produce a breakthrough. In general, it is much easier for people to set a goal than it is to face reality with respect to where they are now, so this part of the process is extremely important in seeing whether the goals are realistic in the first place, as well as in creating a path to the result. The "What's So" process is also used to determine course corrections when people are making efforts toward goals but not getting anywhere, and assuming that doing the same thing will get them different results.

Impossible Future: An Impossible Future is one that challenges existing beliefs about the upward limit of what's possible. An Impossible Future is aspirational, realizable, and becomes the big game in which everyone in the organization can play a meaningful role.

Mastery Versus Competence: In today's (tomorrow's) hypercompetitive job market, having a highly successful career will increasingly require going beyond mere competence to mastery at something. Mastery means being passionate about what you are doing, talented at it beyond the recognizable norm, and able to produce results no matter what. It means doing whatever you do at 100 percent, with skill and artistry, and seeing what you produce as a reflection of your perfect self.

Passionate, Talented A Players in Every Job: In most cases, accomplishing something extraordinary requires *great* players, not just *good* players. Often leaders do not face up to this because it means spending more time getting the right people in the right jobs and coaching them, as well as making some tough people decisions. An A player is someone who shows leadership and collaboration skills above and beyond the ordinary. B's show good leadership and good performance. Chronic C's show poor performance.

Significant Business Challenge: People create a significant business challenge in service of the Impossible Future or strategic challenges and major milestones of the organization. A significant business challenge is an exciting business goal or high-impact project that is a challenge and that makes a difference.

Significant Leadership Challenge: We ask people to create a significant leadership challenge based on who they need to be as a leader to achieve their significant business challenge. A significant leadership challenge represents achieving something as a leader that may require reinventing the business, and, what is more important, reinventing oneself.

Situation: In the course of reaching goals and intentions, people are often presented with situations that represent difficult facts and circumstances. Coaching involves listening to the person's perception of the situation and the issues and dilemmas presented by it in a supportive but also challenging way. It also involves getting people to step back and see the big picture so they gain perspective, as well as providing teachable points of view and templates for action.

Source Document or Blueprint for the Future: Leaders must not only have a vision, they must infect others with it. This can be initiated in conversations with one or more people. However, conversations disappear. A Source Document is an artifact that provides in one place a vision of what the future will be and a plan for how to realize it. A Source Document contains a vision, major goals and milestones, teachable points of view to shape behavior, and key change initiatives, guiding principles, and methodologies.

Source: A leader who originates. Any individual who initiates. A strongly sourced organization is one where an inspiring, empowering leader creates an innovative business concept, a powerful and unique management culture, and an exceptional track record of results.

Structure for Fulfillment: The design or plan and means by which an Impossible Future or any stretch goal can be fulfilled. A structure for fulfillment is created by asking: "What will success look like? What missing pieces of the puzzle need to be put in place and in what arrangement? How do we deploy for action? Who are the key relationships?"

Successful Business Model: A business model is a theory of business put into practice. It is based on beliefs and assumptions about markets, customer needs, and organization capabilities that may prove true or false. The acid test of a successful business model is whether or not it produces profitable growth on a sustainable basis. In coaching, we discover that business leaders often stay in denial, arrogance, or nostalgia long after a once-successful business model has reached the point of diminishing returns. We advocate that at such times it might be more effective to engage in creative destruction and business concept innovation than to tinker with an existing model.

Teachable Point of View: A teachable point of view (TPOV) is often based on golden nuggets, bits of wisdom, or new distinctions that a leader or coach learns through experience and that can be offered in a given situation. Providing a TPOV can involve making new distinctions that have the power to alter people's way of being, reframe thinking, and shift action. For example: You need to make the shift from being an administrator to being a leader. To grow your business, focus on getting different rather than getting better. Seek a career, not just a job.

Template for Action: When people are provided with a TPOV that gets them to think differently, they often start to act differently. A template for action is something we provide in this book to offer people a powerful assist in redesigning their actions. In the end it's a list of how to get started, how to sustain the effort, and things to avoid.

Thinking Partner: A thinking partner is an individual with whom you can create goals, establish realistic plans, and deal with all the situations and dilemmas involved in realizing them. A thinking partner's role is to listen and ask provocative questions that challenge underlying assumptions, as well as to brainstorm alternatives that might represent inventive and effective solutions in dealing with them.

Transactional Leadership: A transactional leader gains compliance from people through carrots and sticks—pay for doing a good job and penalties for noncompliance. A transactional leader is one that attempts to move an agenda forward by doing "deals" with employees, customers, and competitors. A transactional leader often winds up creating something *bigger,* such as a merged company, not necessarily something *better.* Effective leadership often requires both transactional and transformational skills.

Transformational Leadership: A transformational leader is one who not only offers a vision or noble and mighty purpose but also makes believers of people by speaking to their unmet human needs and wants. People come to work and give their all out of a commitment to a higher cause, not just to get a paycheck or avoid punishment. A transformational leader sees an opportunity to make a difference and dares to take a stand, mobilizing people to bring about irreversible change.

Triple-Loop Learning: People who seek to reach goals and bring about change often produce unintended results. Learning occurs when people are able to correct their actions and produce intended results for the first time. Single loop learning involves trying to alter your behavior or do the same thing better. Double loop learning is based on the premise that you need to change your thinking if you want to change your behavior. Triple loop learning involves altering the historical background that shapes people's habitual way of being, thinking, and behavior. Generally, the only way people can overcome the past is through the power of a declaration: I am committed to the possibility of . . . ; I am committed to giving up . . .

Winning Strategy: A winning strategy is the source of an individual's (or enterprise's) success, which at some point becomes a source of limitations. People (and organizations) don't just have a winning strategy, they become their winning strategy. Coaching involves helping people distinguish themselves from their winning strategy so they can create an Impossible Future. This starts with helping people declare goals that they cannot realize within their winning strategy. We ask, Are you willing to put aside the success you have become in order to create an Impossible Future for yourself or your organization?

Acknowledgments

We would like to acknowledge all leaders who have inspired others to make a difference, as well our own coaches, teachers, and mentors, such as Peter Caddy, Michio Kushi, and Joan Holmes.

We would like to acknowledge Susan Youngquist (Robert's wife) for the miraculous job she played as "Big City Editor" on *Your Coach (In a Book)*. She offered a powerful assist in picking relevant scenarios and handing out the assignments to staff writers Robert and Michel. She also provided a good balance of inspiration to keep at it and tough, cigar-chomping, no-monkey-business editing (puzzle solving). "Hello Susan, here is what I just wrote. Brilliant, isn't it?" Thirty minutes later, "No, it's crap! Revise it again! And by the way, it's got to come down from ten pages to seven. Arrggh!"

We would also like to acknowledge Veronica Pemberton (Michel's wife) for the role she played in this work. Her ability to articulate inspiring ideas, make distinctions that open new possibilities in people's minds, and turn a phrase was greatly appreciated.

We would also like to acknowledge those people who have generously empowered us to coach them and thus advance our skills, capabilities, and state of the art. First, we would like to acknowledge Greg Goff, one of the best people we have coached, a fabulous thinking partner and the source of some key ideas in this book, including the distinction of the "significant leadership and business challenges." Others who were actively involved with us during the months we were writing this book were Richard Severance, Jim Nokes, Barry Kumins, Bob Hassler, Chris Head, Jenny Baker, Tom Souls, John Young, and Fulvio Bussandri.

We would like to acknowledge Tom Peters, author of *Re-Imagine! Business Excellence in a Disruptive Age,* for the get-up-in-the-morning inspiration of his writing style, which is like a cup of strong black coffee. We admire his ability to present powerful, provocative, and world-shaking ideas in an exuberant, fast-paced, yet down-to-earth way. We would also like to acknowledge Gary Hamel, author of *Leading the Revolution: How to Survive in Turbulent Times by Making Innovation a Way of Life,* for the inspiration of his writing style and his contribution to our thinking about the need for strategic resilience and business concept innovation in every enterprise today.

About the Authors

Robert Hargrove is chairman of Masterful Coaching, Inc., of Brookline, Massachusetts. He is a former director of the Harvard Leadership Research Project. The focus of his work is on inspiring and empowering executive leaders in business, government, health care, education, the arts, and science to make a difference in their world. He also works with emerging leaders who represent the future.

Hargrove is the author of *Masterful Coaching, Mastering the Art of Creative Collaboration, E-Leader,* and other books. He has developed "Masterful Coaching, the Executive Coaching Method," which is widely recognized by leading authorities as the fastest, most powerful, and most profound way to produce extraordinary leaders and extraordinary results.

Hargrove's work usually involves a one-year coaching program that involves working with leaders to set and realize a significant business and leadership challenge. The process provides real-time coaching on emerging issues, as well as insightful 360-degree feedback.

Michel Renaud is a senior partner in Masterful Coaching and lives in Montreal, Canada. Renaud has played a pivotal and decisive role in contributing groundbreaking insights based on his coaching experiences with executives at all levels in businesses and NGOs that are the foundation of the work at Masterful Coaching, Inc.

Renaud is the mastermind behind the highly acclaimed "Action Coaching" program, which is for people in groups. The program is designed to achieve a business breakthrough, a leadership breakthrough, a team breakthrough, and a coaching environment where people promote one another's success.

Please contact Robert Hargrove or Michel Renaud at 617-739-3302 or by e-mail at Robert.Hargrove@MasterfulCoaching.com or Michel.Renaud@MasterfulCoaching.com.

Index